A Child's Journey

The Christian Initiation of Children

Rita Burns Senseman

ST. ANTHONY MESSENGER PRESS
Cincinnati, Ohio

■ *To Sarah Burns, Katherine Alice and Rachel Marie*

Nihil obstat: Rev. Ralph J. Lawrence
　　　　　　Rev. Donald Miller, O.F.M.

Imprimi Potest: Rev. John Bok, O.F.M.
　　　　　　Provincial

Imprimatur: Rev. Carl K. Moeddel,
　　　　　　Vicar General
　　　　　　Archdiocese of Cincinnati
　　　　　　September 22, 1997

The nihil obstat and imprimatur are a declaration that a book or pamphlet is considered to be free of doctrinal or moral error. It is not implied that those who have granted the nihil obstat or imprimatur agree with the contents, opinions or statements expressed.

Excerpts from the English translation of *Rite of Christian Initiation of Adults* copyright ©1985, International Commission on English in the Liturgy. All rights reserved.

Cover design by Mary Alfieri
Cover illustration by Mary Newell DePalma
Book design by Sandy L. Digman
Electronic pagination and format by Sandy L. Digman

ISBN 0-86716-264-3

Published by St. Anthony Messenger Press
www.AmericanCatholic.org
Printed in the U.S.A.

Contents

Acknowledgments

The children and families who have shared their stories with me have made this book possible. I am grateful to all those who allowed me to journey with them in the process of Christian initiation. I am privileged to have walked with them for a while, and they have graced my life tremendously.

Many others have also walked with me, helping me along the way. First, I would like to acknowledge the North American Forum on the Catechumenate. The people who make up the Forum have greatly influenced my thinking on Christian initiation. Most important, they have taught me to be faithful to the essential and primary text of Christian initiation, the *Rite of Christian Initiation of Adults*. Since I first attended a North American Forum Beginnings and Beyond Institute in July 1985, I have been learning how to implement the Rite. The people of Forum have helped me study and interpret the Rite. I am also grateful to the people of St. Andrew the Apostle Parish in Indianapolis for sending me to that first institute and for first inviting me to begin this approach to initiation ministry in their parish.

The methods used throughout the sample sessions are based on some of the examples and methods offered by the North American Forum, adapted for use with children and families.

I wish to thank two members of the North American Forum who have particularly influenced me and supported my work: Maureen Kelly and Bob Duggan. They have been and continue to be my mentors. Maureen has been a source of edification and encouragement for me. Consultations and discussions with her have helped me clarify my thinking on the Christian initiation of children and challenged me to modify my pastoral practice. Likewise, Bob Duggan has graciously and generously shared his time and expertise with me. He has critiqued my work and ministry and suggested to me new ways of looking at Christian initiation. His consultations provided me with new insights and greater knowledge of the *Rite of Christian Initiation of Adults*.

The late Jim Dunning, cofounder of the North American Forum on the Catechumenate, has also significantly influenced my thinking, particularly in his work *Echoing God's Word: Formation for Catechists and Homilists in a Catechumenal Church*. You will find elements of his work echoed throughout this volume.

The Rev. Frederick C. Easton, J.C.L., vicar judicial for the Archdiocese of Indianapolis, provided consultation on matters involving Church law. I appreciate the time he spent discussing questions with me and the effort he put into researching the answers to those questions.

Claudia Givinsky of Warren, Michigan, also spent a great deal of time editing my work and offering insightful and helpful suggestions. I am grateful not only for her critique, but for the vision, compassion and friendship she has shown to me throughout the past several years.

I also wish to give credit to Linda Gaupin for her work in the area of sacramental catechesis. The materials on sacramental catechesis in Chapter Four are based on ideas she presented at a catechetical seminar for the Archdiocese of Detroit.

Lastly, I extend my heartfelt thanks to the women of the Oakbay Babysitting Co-Op and my sisters, Laura Yeakey and Bess Howes, for the loving care they gave to Sarah and Katherine while I was writing. I am forever grateful to all the people who have been part of my wondrous journey.

Rita Burns Senseman
31 May 1996
The Visitation of Mary to Elizabeth

Introduction

I thought I knew a lot about children. And, I thought I had a passion for the ministry of Christian initiation, particularly with children and families. But, not until I had children of my own did I realize what great truth is contained in the *Rite of Christian Initiation of Adults*, which envisions children as persons who are capable of a journey of conversion that leads to deeper relationship with the living God. Though I "knew" this truth before, now that I have two daughters of my own, I see it more completely. I see firsthand how children come to develop a relationship with God, how God's word touches them, how stories and symbols carry meaning for children, how family is central for children and how deeply spiritual children really are.

Although my daughters are still young, (Sarah is two and a half and Katherine is only ten months), they have convinced me that a child's initiation into the faith community is a journey of conversion for both the child and the family. Indeed, that is the vision of Christian initiation found in the *Rite of Christian Initiation of Adults* and presented in this book.

This book is designed for parish ministers involved in Christian initiation, particularly those catechists and initiation coordinators who specialize in the initiation process for children of catechetical age. I also believe that this book will be helpful for liturgists, pastors, presiders of the liturgical rites and other initiation team members. It takes as its point of departure the *Rite of Christian Initiation of Adults*. Its purpose is to guide those who pastorally implement the *Rite of Christian Initiation of Adults* as it is adapted for children

of catechetical age. It is my hope that this book will be useful both to those with experience in initiation ministry and to those who have little experience with the initiation of children.

Though many parishes are implementing the *Rite of Christian Initiation of Adults*, they always find that new challenges and questions arise when they adapt the Rite to children of catechetical age. This book will examine the special issues and will attempt to provide solid, practical approaches for dealing with them.

Pastoral ministers need practical advice. Few have the time or energy to puzzle out all the answers all by themselves. And why should they? Part of being Church is about helping each other on our common journey. The insights, approaches and methods I offer come from my own pastoral experience. I've been involved with the Christian initiation of children for more than ten years in small, large, city and suburban parishes. The anecdotes I give throughout the book are true. Names have been changed, and occasionally the story has been modified to emphasize or clarify a particular point. Likewise, the questions I address throughout the book are real questions that I have encountered along the way.

One of the most frequently asked questions is, "What do you 'use' for initiation of children of catechetical age?" My unequivocal answer is the *Rite of Christian Initiation of Adults*. Therefore, in order to understand how to approach the initiation of children of catechetical age, you should have a copy of, and be familiar with, the *Rite of Christian Initiation of Adults* ("the Rite").[1]

Before you begin, here are several other important points that may need some clarification: First, the Rite is designed for the initiation of children of catechetical age, which the Church generally considers to be seven to fourteen years. There are, however, many exceptions to this norm. I also recognize that children reach adolescence before their fourteenth year, but rather than continually saying "children and adolescents," I'll use the word children to refer to those between the ages of seven and fourteen.

Also, when referring to those who are in the process of initiation, the terms *catechumen* and *candidate* are often used. A catechumen is a person who is not baptized but is seeking baptism and has entered the period of the catechumenate. Generally, a candidate is a baptized person preparing for full initiation. Be aware that the Rite itself uses the term *candidate* to refer to any person, baptized or unbaptized, who is in the process of initiation (that is, a candidate for initiation). In this book, I will usually use the term *candidate* to refer to a child, baptized or unbaptized, who is in the process of initiation. However, when referring to the periods of Evangelization and the Precatechumenate, Catechumenate, Purification and Enlightenment, I will also use the terms *inquirer*, *catechumen* and *elect*, respectively, to refer to those who are not baptized. The term *neophyte* refers to one who is newly baptized.

Lastly, great attention is given to the liturgical rites and the process of liturgical catechesis because they are paramount throughout the initiation process.

The sample sessions in this book are real in the sense that I have used them myself at various times and in various parishes. They are meant to give you a picture of what a precatechumenate or catechumenate or mystagogical session might look like. The sample sessions are not meant to be scripts or lessons plans for you to use verbatim. You must design your own sessions because they must be tailored to fit the needs, ages and maturity of your candidates. Use the samples as thought-starters or outlines, and then adapt them to fit the needs of your candidates.

The catechetical method used in the sample sessions is heavily influenced by Thomas Groome's "Shared Christian Praxis." The emphasis in Groome's method is on using human experience as the point of departure for faith formation.

If you are coming to this text using only the lens of catechesis and religious education, I would like to challenge you to change your paradigm. This book is not about the religious education of children. And it is not about another religious education or sacramental preparation program. It is about conversion. Though catechesis is certainly a part of the formation of young catechumens and candidates, Christian initiation is a journey of conversion that transforms children and their families.

Those of us who have the honor of sharing most intimately in the journey of the children and their families are privileged to witness grace in action. This book will help those who share the journey with children and their families to dare to let the Spirit lead.

REFERENCES

[1] The *Rite of Christian Initiation of Adults, Study Edition*, Approved for use in the dioceses of the United States by the National Conference of Catholic Bishops and confirmed by the Holy See. Prepared by the International Commission on English in the Liturgy and the Bishops Committee on the Liturgy (Chicago: Liturgy Training Publications, 1988). Those who do not have a copy of the Rite may ask parish staff members for a copy or obtain a copy from their local Catholic bookstore or any number of publishers, including Liturgy Training Publications, 1-800-933-1800.

1

The Vision

Darlene Stipes telephoned the parish office asking for her children to be baptized. Stacy was twelve and Michael was ten. "We've recently started coming to church again and my kids have never been baptized," explained Darlene. Later, Darlene described how she had been reared in a "strong Catholic" family and she now felt that her children needed a church that provided them with the kind of "home base" she had known as a child. Darlene had recently been through a divorce and was feeling as though she needed to connect with her "home base" again, too.

Darlene and her children made an initial commitment to participate in the process of initiation at St. Margaret Parish. For various reasons, their participation waxed and waned. After the first year, they decided they wanted to get more serious about their commitment, and they began to enter more fully into the process. In one of the final pastoral interviews before their initiation, Stacy described their family this way: "It's like our family is happier. Mom and Dad are back together. We don't fight as much. And I like coming to church."

The Stipes family story is one of the many examples of the types of families and children who come to the Catholic Church seeking initiation. Their reasons for coming are many. Their situations, desires and motives are as diverse as the families and children themselves.

Because the children are of catechetical age, they must be fully initiated according to the Rite of Christian Initiation of Adults. The vision of the Rite is that children's initiation is a rich, transforming experience. I believe that vision contains four main elements:

- children are to be initiated for mission;
- children are to experience conversion through the process;
- children are to be initiated within the paschal mystery;
- children are to be initiated in and through the faith community and their families.

Elements of the Vision

Initiated for Mission

Through sacramental initiation, children become part of the Body of Christ. By virtue of their baptism, children share in the death, resurrection and glorification of Jesus Christ. Sharing in Jesus' life, death, resurrection and glorification includes sharing in his mission. As disciples of Jesus, the baptized continue his mission on earth.

The "General Introduction" to the Rite (#2) describes the culmination of sacramental initiation as bringing "us, the faithful of Christ, to his full stature and to enable us to carry out the mission of the entire people of God in the Church and in the world." Clearly, initiation is focused more on discipleship than on membership. The grace of the sacraments makes the newly initiated more like Jesus Christ, with a share in his mission. The emphasis is not on "making good Catholics," but on forming disciples of Jesus Christ who continue his work of furthering the Reign of God.

Since children are as much a part of the faithful as are adults, they too have a responsibility to carry out the mission of the people of God. They do this in their families, in their schools and on their playgrounds; at their sporting events and recitals; in the malls and video arcades; with their peers; with their families and in every aspect of their world. Finding and modeling concrete ways in which children can fulfill this responsibility is a part of their formation as disciples and part of our responsibility as their pastoral guides.

Conversion

Becoming a disciple of Jesus Christ requires conversion. The vision of the *Rite of Christian Initiation of Adults* is that the initiation of children as well as adults is a process of conversion. For example, the Stipes family undoubtedly experienced conversion. They moved from being a disjointed and searching family to a unified, rooted, faith-filled, worshiping family. Stacy, a withdrawn young person lacking self-confidence, became a rather animated, self-confident adolescent able to express a living faith. Michael's conversion manifested itself most concretely in the cheerful, helpful attitude he developed toward his family and neighbors. Darlene also testified that the family's journey of conversion included the resolution of her marriage problems.

The "General Introduction on Christian Initiation" and the "Introduction" to the *Rite of*

Christian Initiation of Adults, which are both found in the ritual text, refer to conversion as the vision of Christian initiation. The opening paragraph of the "General Introduction" states that "in the sacraments of Christian Initiation we are freed from the power of darkness and joined to Christ's death, burial and resurrection." For children and their families, this means that initiation frees them from whatever keeps them in darkness, and unites them to Jesus Christ. Sacramental initiation promises them that the power of the paschal mystery is theirs.

Similarly, the "Introduction" to the *Rite of Christian Initiation of Adults* says that those who desire initiation "seek the living God and enter the way of faith and conversion as the Holy Spirit opens their hearts" (#1).

A longing for a relationship with God and a change of heart are at the center of the initiation process. Initiation is not primarily "learning everything you ever wanted to know about being a Catholic." Initiation is about deepening one's relationship with the living God. It is about changing one's attitude, actions and life-style and becoming more like Jesus Christ.

The *Rite of Christian Initiation of Adults* specifically refers to both conversion and children: "The Christian initiation of these children requires both a conversion that is personal and somewhat developed, in proportion to their age" (#253). A "personal" conversion is one in which the child as a unique individual is truly changed by the power of grace and the witness of the Christian community. Although the process of initiation includes the entire family, the child is the focal point of the conversion process. Thus, the child's "personal" conversion means that the community looks for a change not only in the family as a whole, but in the life of the individual child.

Secondly, a conversion that is "somewhat

developed, in proportion to their age," refers to a conversion that is significant, yet developmentally appropriate. A "somewhat developed" conversion is one that affects various dimensions—affective, intellectual, moral and social—of the child's life. The important point here is to acknowledge that a child is capable of conversion. The Rite certainly acknowledges this when it describes the children as being "capable of receiving and nurturing a personal faith and of recognizing an obligation in conscience" (#252). Children in the process of initiation are those who are mature enough to be formed in faith and to enter into a conversion process. Certainly conversion differs depending on the maturity level of the child, just as conversion differs for each adult.

Another way of describing the process of conversion for children is to see initiation as a spiritual journey rather than a program of religious education. Many families who bring their children for initiation believe that what their children really need is religious instruction in order to "get baptized." Many parents feel that their child has "missed out" or is "out of step." The Rite, however, says that "initiation is suited to a spiritual journey of adults that varies according to the many forms of God's grace, the free cooperation of the individuals, the action of the Church, and the circumstances of time and place" (#5). Children seeking initiation, then, are not "out of step." The Spirit has led them to the parish at this particular time in their lives. The child's relationship with God and the community is the most important aspect of the journey to initiation.

Although suitable religious instruction, or catechesis, is part of the process, initiation is meant to be primarily a journey of faith. The journey will be different for each child and for each family, depending on the questions and the needs of the family and "depending on the many forms of God's grace." Each child comes with a different family history and with different needs. The process of initiation, then, needs to be flexible and adaptable in order to allow freedom for each child's faith journey.

In addition, the faith journey of each child will progress differently. The Stipes family's journey, for instance, moved along quite slowly. Their participation in the parish process of initiation was sporadic at times. Nonetheless, God was working in their lives, and when the time was right, they became committed to the parish community and the initiation process.

For some children and their families the journey of initiation may be extended over several years; for others it may last only a short time. According to the Rite, "The initiation of catechumens is a gradual process" (#4). And, children's "initiation is to be extended over several years, if need be, before they receive the sacraments" (#253).

The spiritual journey of each child, then, is a process of conversion that should be gradual and unhurried. It should be accommodated to the needs of each child and her or his family. And, it should comprise elements of formation as well as elements of information or religious instruction.

Paschal Mystery

At the center of the process of conversion is the paschal mystery. In the process of initiation, the children come to a deeper understanding of the meaning of Christ's life, death, resurrection and glorification. When talking about Jesus' passion and death, thirteen-year-old Stephanie, another catechumen at St. Margaret Parish, said, "He must love us an awful lot. I don't know if I could go through that."

Part of the vision of the Rite is that the

candidates for initiation—adults as well as children—will make connections between the paschal mystery (Jesus' life, death, resurrection and glorification) and their own lives. The process of initiation leads candidates to ask the big questions about Jesus Christ and about God's love for us. For example, on the Solemnity of Christ the King, Stephanie, who was particularly intrigued with Jesus' suffering, asked, "So, why did Jesus die, anyway?"

Questions like that provide a point of departure for leading children to an appreciation of the value and meaning of the paschal mystery in their own lives. All children have had some experience with death—be it the death of a loved one or favorite pet, the illness of friend or relative, loss through divorce or some other major life change. This can be a place to begin to catechize them about our Christian belief in resurrection. Throughout their journeys, they come to see how their stories of death and life are intimately "joined to the death, burial, and resurrection" of Christ Jesus ("General Introduction," #1).

Community and Family

Reflection on the value and meaning of the paschal mystery takes place within the community of the faithful (#4). Children's first experience of community is their family. The *Rite of Christian Initiation of Adults* is clear about the centrality of the family in the process of initiation for children. Children are "dependent" upon their parents or guardians (#252, 254). The Rite expresses a "hope" that the children will "receive as much help and example as possible from their parents, whose permission is required for the children to be initiated and to live the Christian life" (#254.2).

Indeed, if a child is to experience conversion, the child's entire family will undoubtedly be influenced and affected by such a change in the life of a child. Although there are certainly times when parents and families cannot be involved in the process of initiation, the vision of the Rite is that they have a pivotal role in the children's journey to conversion. In other words, the process of initiation for children is family-centered. The family is to be intimately and actively involved with the child throughout the entire process. The family participates in formation sessions with the child. The parents participate in all the liturgical rites as well, for the parent is the child's sponsor and presents the child for each of the rites (#260). In the instances when a parent cannot be involved in the process, a sponsor takes the place of the parent.

In addition, the vision of the Rite of Christian Initiation of Adults is that the children and their families walk on the journey of faith together with other families and with members of the community. Initiation is to take place "within the supportive setting" of baptized companions (#254). The Church envisions the spiritual journey of the candidates being supported by the living and active faith of the children's peers. They will benefit from the companionship of baptized children of their own age. More will be said about these peers in subsequent chapters.

Furthermore, the Rite emphasizes that initiation is the responsibility of all the baptized (#9). Children who seek initiation are surrounded not only by their families, sponsors and companions but they are also formed in faith by the entire community. Opportunities for the children and their families to interact with the parish community are an important aspect of the Church's vision of initiation. One of the most significant ways the community forms, supports and prays for the candidates is through the celebration of the liturgical rites.

The Liturgical Rites and the Vision of Christian Initiation

The *Rite of Christian Initiation of Adults* is a liturgical *ordo*, or order, that includes a series of separate but interrelated rites, both major and minor. The major rites are celebrated at the culmination of each period of the initiation process. Likewise, each of the major rites points to, or anticipates, the next period in the process. The rites serve as "doorways" through which the candidates pass as they proceed to the next stages, or periods, in the initiation process (#6).

The Rite of Christian Initiation of Adults is divided into four periods and contains three major liturgical rites. The periods are:

1. evangelization and precatechumenate;
2. the catechumenate;
3. purification and enlightenment;
4. postbaptismal catechesis, or mystagogy.

The three major liturgical rites are:

1. Rite of Acceptance Into the Order of Catechumens;
2. Rite of Election;
3. the Sacraments of Initiation—Baptism, Confirmation, Eucharist.

The liturgical rites are foundational in the vision of Christian initiation. Not only are they a summation and culmination of each period of the initiation process, but they are also highly significant moments in the formation of the candidates. For children especially, the rituals speak at a level that verbal language cannot. The signs and symbols, the sights and sounds, the gestures, prayers, processions, music and movement engage children in a profound way. The rituals express the mystery of the Holy One alive and working in the community. The liturgical rites are key to—and have the utmost priority in—the process of

initiation. Parish initiation teams would do well to read, study and reflect on these rites as a major part of team formation.

Each of the major rites has a particular focus and purpose in and of itself as well as for the periods that surround it.

The Period of Evangelization and Precatechumenate

The first period of the process of initiation is that of evangelization and precatechumenate. During the evangelization period, the living God is "faithfully and constantly" proclaimed (#36). The Rite of Acceptance Into the Order of Catechumens, which is the culmination of this first period, indicates that during the precatechumenate the children have become acquainted with the all-loving God and Jesus Christ.

The Rite of Acceptance implies that in the preceding period, the children have become familiar with God's word and with the Christian way of life, which includes an acceptance of the cross. The primary means by which children do this is through the sharing of stories. The children's and families' stories are connected with God's story and with the story of the Christian community. Once initial conversion has occurred and the child expresses a desire to continue the journey of faith, the Rite of Acceptance into the Order of Catechumens is celebrated.

The Rite of Acceptance Into the Order of Catechumens

This first major liturgical rite marks the end of the first period and the beginning of the second, the catechumenate proper. The Rite of Acceptance Into the Order of Catechumens

7

celebrates the initial conversion of the children and the first public welcome of the candidates to the Church. The children declare their intention to become members of the Church, and the Church "marks their reception and first consecration" (#41).

The Period of the Catechumenate

The period of the catechumenate is a time to deepen the child catechumen's initial conversion by means of "suitable pastoral formation" (#75). This formation includes a "suitable catechesis based on the word of God and accommodated to the liturgical year" (#75.1); familiarity with the Christian way of life through interaction with the community; liturgical rites, such as celebrations of the word of God, blessings, exorcisms and anointings; participation in service to the community. Once again, the Rite of Acceptance Into the Order of Catechumens indicates that the word of God will have prominence in the upcoming period of the catechumenate.

Once the child has "undergone conversion in mind and in action" and has "developed a sufficient acquaintance with Christian teaching" (#120), the child takes the second step in the initiation process and celebrates the Rite of Election.

The Rite of Election

Although the *Rite of Christian Initiation of Adults* indicates that this liturgical rite is optional for children (#277), most parishes include the children in this rite, which closes the period of the catechumenate proper and begins the "final, more intense preparation for the sacraments of initiation" (#118). The rite itself is the celebration of God's election, or choice, of the children as expressed through

the voice of the Church, specifically through the bishop or his designated representative. The Rite of Election acknowledges the conversion that has taken place, and it anticipates the continuing conversion that will happen in the third period.

The Period of Purification and Enlightenment

The third period is a time of "intense spiritual preparation" for the children and their families (#138). It is the proximate preparation for the celebration of the sacraments of initiation. The liturgical rites of this period, especially the Scrutinies, which are solemn liturgical ceremonies of introspection and repentance, and the handing over of the Creed and Lord's Prayer are the primary means of formation for the children. The period ordinarily coincides with the season of Lent, the forty-day "retreat" that serves as the final preparation for the celebration of the paschal mystery.

Celebration of the Sacraments of Initiation

The third and final step of the initiation process for the children is the celebration of the sacraments of Baptism, Confirmation and Eucharist. Except in unusual circumstances, this celebration takes place at the Easter Vigil. The *Rite of Christian Initiation of Adults* is clear that children of catechetical age receive the three sacraments of initiation at the same celebration (#305, National Statute 18). Children celebrate the fullness of sacramental initiation. Confirmation and Eucharist are not to be delayed.

Period of Postbaptismal Catechesis or Mystagogy

The final period of the children's initiation is the period of postbaptismal catechesis, or mystagogy. This is the time for the children to reflect upon the great mysteries celebrated during their journey to initiation. By meditating on the gospel, sharing in the Eucharist, doing works of charity and reflecting upon their experiences of the liturgical rites, the children come to deepen "their grasp of the paschal mystery" (#330, 244). In addition, the so-called Neophyte Masses and the lectionary readings of the Easter season provide a focus for the children. Also, this is the time for the children to make the final transition into the community of the faithful and to become more at home with their previously baptized peers. Full incorporation into the parish catechetical program is also a part of this transition.

Liturgical Catechesis

The liturgical rites are pivotal points in the initiation process for children. The *Rite of Christian Initiation of Adults* envisions liturgical catechesis as a key part of the process. Although "liturgical catechesis," per se, is specifically mentioned only once in the Rite (#138), the vision is that the entire process of Christian formation be grounded in and lead to the liturgy—be that the eucharistic liturgy of the Easter Vigil, the Sunday liturgies of the word or the minor rites of the catechumenate.

Liturgical catechesis in and of itself has not yet been clearly defined. Experts in liturgy, catechesis and initiation ministry are wrestling with its full meaning.[1] However, a brief description here may help you put in context the centrality of liturgical catechesis for the Christian initiation of children.

In general, liturgical catechesis is the catechetical activity that surrounds a liturgical ritual as well as the ritual activity itself. That is, it comprises all the catechetical activity that prepares for and leads to a liturgical celebration, the liturgical ritual itself, and all the catechetical activity following a liturgical celebration that deliberately "unpacks" its meaning.[2] Since the liturgy itself is a formative experience that deepens and strengthens faith, the liturgical rituals of the initiation process are the pivots around which all the catechetical activity in Christian initiation moves. Moreover, the lectionary readings, as part of the Liturgy of the Word, are an important aspect of liturgical catechesis. Candidates for initiation are always moving toward, through or away from a ritual celebration.

Further, for children in the initiation process, liturgical catechesis means that liturgical symbols are to be used frequently, correctly, robustly and reverently throughout the process. Liturgical catechesis includes reflection on the primary symbols of all the rites celebrated before they are celebrated. This is especially true for the major rites. Likewise, the symbols are unpacked and the readings are "broken open" following the celebration of the liturgies. Also, liturgical catechesis includes catechesis for children that leads them to the assembly's liturgical celebration of God's word each Sunday and thereafter breaks open the meaning of that word in their young lives.

Liturgical catechesis, then, is a catechetical process that has three movements and two primary elements. The three movements are:

1. the preparation for the liturgical experience;
2. the liturgical experience itself;
3. the unpacking of the meaning of the liturgical experience.

The two primary elements of the catechetical process are:

1. the lectionary readings of the liturgical celebration;
2. the ritual symbols (which include ritual actions) of the celebration.

The liturgy's word and symbols are the points of departure for both preparation and reflection sessions (see diagram below). The practical implementation of liturgical catechesis for the initiation of children will be discussed in later chapters.

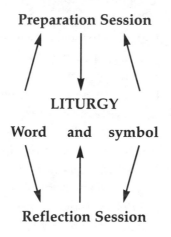

Preparation Session

LITURGY

Word   and   symbol

Reflection Session

The Normative Means of Christian Initiation

The *Rite of Christian Initiation of Adults* is the normal means by which children of catechetical age are initiated. The Rite addresses both the initiation of adults and the initiation of children of catechetical age. Part I of the Rite is designed for adults who have not been baptized and seek full initiation. The first section of Part II of the Rite is designed for children of catechetical age who have not been baptized and likewise seek full initiation. (Other special situations exist in which

baptized children also follow the norms of the Rite. These situations will be discussed in the next chapter.)

The National Statutes on the Catechumenate, issued by the United States bishops, in the section entitled "Children of Catechetical Age," says that "since children who have reached the use of reason are considered, for purposes of Christian initiation, to be adults (canon 852:1), their formation should follow the general pattern of the ordinary catechumenate as far as possible, with the appropriate adaptations permitted by the ritual" (National Statute 18). In other words, what is said in Part I of the Rite regarding adults is applicable to children, although it is to be adapted in developmentally appropriate ways.

At this point, then, what is most important to understand is that Part I of the *Rite of Christian Initiation of Adults* presents the norm for initiation of adults and children of catechetical age, and it contains the vision of the initiation process for everyone involved. Part II of the Rite, "Rites for Particular Circumstances," is an adaptation of Part I. This adaptation was put together hastily because the liturgists developing the Rite presumed that the adaptation would not be used much. Because of this hurried construction, inconsistencies exist between Parts I and II. If you minister in the initiation of children, it is important that you grasp this reality. It is also vital that you understand that when inconsistencies occur, Part I, which describes normative initiation, always takes precedence.

Another important consideration regarding Parts I and II of the Rite is the unity of the entire ritual text and of the overall process of Christian initiation. While there will be times when children and adults meet separately, only one process of initiation exists for both children and adults.

Furthermore, there is no such ritual text

commonly referred to as the "RCIC" (Rite of Christian Initiation of Children) or the "OCIC" (Order of Christian Initiation of Children). Only two rites exist in the Church that deal with the initiation of children into the Christian community: the Rite of Baptism for Children (for children younger than the age of reason—about age seven) and the Rite of Christian Initiation of Adults (for adults and for children who have reached the age of reason).

REFERENCES

[1] For example, see Thomas Morris, "Liturgical Catechesis Revisited," *Catechumenate: A Journal of Christian Initiation*, May 1995.

[2] The basis for this definition comes from a working definition of liturgical catechesis given by Father Bob Duggan at a conference for Region VI Diocesan Directors of Christian Initiation in Adrian, Mich., May 1993.

Summary

Knowing, believing and striving to implement the vision of Christian initiation is essential to a successful initiation ministry for children. If you are or wish to be involved in the initiation ministry for children, and if you understand children's formation as only a catechetical, or instructional, model, then you must shift your understanding to that of an initiation model.

The process of initiation as envisioned in the Rite of Christian Initiation of Adults leads children into discipleship with Jesus Christ. Becoming a disciple is a journey of conversion centered in the paschal mystery. Conversion to the person and mission of Jesus Christ is at the heart of the initiation process. Because conversion is expected of children involved in this process, it is often experienced in the family as well. The entire process of initiation is family-centered and liturgical catechesis is the normal means of formation.

Notes

2

The Children and Their Families

Ever since he had entered first grade at St. Anthony School, Stephen Owens had been telling his parents that he wanted to "be a Catholic." Stephen was now in third grade, and his parents decided that his desire to be Catholic was something they should take seriously. Stephen's parents first talked to his teacher, then to the school principal, and then to the director of religious education. No one was quite sure what to do, but finally, Christine and Steve Owens, along with their son, met with the director of religious education to talk about Stephen's desire for initiation.

Although ninety percent of Stephen's Catholic school classmates were not Catholic, St. Anthony Parish and School were a source of evangelization for Stephen. The children, the teachers, the staff, the environment, the classes and the liturgy had spoken to Stephen about the Good News of Jesus Christ. Christine and Steve Owens told Barbara, the director of religious education, that for two years Stephen had been saying he wanted to be a Catholic. When asked directly, Stephen said he wanted to be Catholic because he liked St. Anthony, he liked religion class and he liked going to church. The strength and depth of his desire were enough to convince his parents and Barbara that his journey to initiation was already under way.

Christine was a Baptist, baptized as a teenager, and, although Steve professed to be a believing Christian, he had never been baptized. The family was not presently involved in any church, though they had been in the past. The Owenses wanted Stephen to make his own decision about faith and religion, and since he was consistently interested in the Catholic faith, they wanted to be supportive of his interest. Although Christine and Steve would give their permission for Stephen to inquire about the Catholic faith, they had no personal interest in the faith themselves. Nonetheless, they agreed to support Stephen by fully participating in the initiation process. A sponsoring family from St. Anthony would later join Stephen and his parents in the process. Eventually, as the Owens family story unfolded, Stephen was fully initiated and his parents later joined their son as Catholic Christians.

Like the inquiring adults who present themselves at our parish doors, children seeking initiation usually represent a mixed group in regard to their backgrounds, their acquaintance with the Catholic Church (or any church) and their family situations. Stephen was unbaptized, but catechized, and his parents were not Catholic. Another child catechumen at St. Anthony was unbaptized, uncatechized and her parents were Catholic. Other children may be baptized candidates for full communion with the Roman Catholic

Church rather than candidates for the catechumenate. Some of the children have parents who are baptized. Others have parents who are not baptized. Some of the parents are Catholic, others are members of another Christian church. Some children come on their own initiative, others come on the urging or insistence of family members. There are a vast number of situations from which child catechumens and candidates come, and there are a vast number of reasons why they come seeking initiation. We will look at some of these situations and possible ways to deal with them.

Children of Catechetical Age

First, we need to be clear about the ages involved in the description "catechetical age."

The *Rite of Christian Initiation of Adults* says that it is for children "who have attained the use of reason and are of catechetical age" (#252). According to the Church's Code of Canon Law (canon 11), the use of reason is attained at approximately seven years of age.[1] However, canon law also recognizes that seven is an arbitrary age. "No precise moment can be detected when a child 'receives' the use of reason and begins to make judgments and decisions."[2]

The Rite does give a helpful clarification, however; it speaks of children being "capable of receiving and nurturing a personal faith and of recognizing an obligation in conscience" (#252). Therefore, if a child is capable of faith formation and conscience formation, then she or he has attained the use of reason.[3]

Significantly, the Rite says the children are to have the use of reason and be "of catechetical age."[4] The Code does not give an approximate age for "catechetical age," the age at which a child is capable of being formed in faith. There is no specific age at which this happens.

On the other hand, the authors of the Rite may have intended catechetical age to mean "school age," which could be five, six or seven years of age. Nonetheless, considering all of the possible meanings of the terms "catechetical age" and "age of reason," the guiding principle seems to be that at approximately age seven a child is of catechetical age and has the use of reason. There are, however, always exceptions to this general rule.

The three children in the Johnson family were all unbaptized candidates for initiation. The children's ages were nine, six, and four years. Four-year-old Jessica was baptized, confirmed and admitted to the Eucharist along with her older sisters. Through a process of discernment, the parents and the initiation team determined that Jessica had attained the use of reason and that she should be fully initiated with her older sisters.

Each child should be given individual consideration when deciding if she or he should follow Part II of the Rite ("Rites for Particular Circumstances").

The Rite itself states that the first section of Part II is for children who have attained the use of reason (#252). Thus, if catechetical age begins at approximately age seven, at what age does it end? When is a person no longer a child of catechetical age? This is an important question, because parental permission is required for a child of catechetical age to be initiated (#252, 254). The question is often asked, "When is parental permission no longer needed in order for a child to be initiated?" Or, "At what age does a person follow Part I of the Rite instead of Part II?"

According to Rev. Frederick C. Easton, J.C.L., vicar judicial of the Metropolitan Tribunal of the Archdiocese of Indianapolis, "Neither the Rite [Rite of Christian Initiation of Adults] nor the Code of Canon Law nor any other ecclesiastical law expressly determines the age when the parental permission is no longer needed."[5] In other words, "The law gives no upper age limit on those who are considered children of catechetical age."[6] However, the Code does address issues related to the question of maximum age and when parental permission is no longer needed for initiation. First, canon 97 states that when a person has completed the eighteenth year, then she or he is no longer a minor. Therefore, those eighteen years and older are no longer children and would not need parental permission for initiation. Those over the age of eighteen would definitely follow Part I of the Rite.

The question of parental permission remains for adolescents younger than eighteen. The Code does make a reference to baptism that could be applied to the question of parental permission for initiation. Canon 863 refers to those over the age of fourteen as adults.[7]

Also, canon 1478.3 says that those who are fourteen can make a decision regarding "spiritual matters" without the consent of their parents. In this canon, "the Code determines that persons who are not yet adults can make certain decisions in their spiritual or ecclesiastical life."[8] John M. Huels also points to canon 111.2, which says that "at age fourteen a person is free to choose to be baptized in any ritual church—in the Latin rite or an Eastern rite."[9] Thus, applying the norms of canons 863, 111.2 and 1478.3 to the question of parental permission for baptism, we can conclude that parental permission is not needed if a child is fourteen. Or, more precisely, "there would be no strictly canonical requirement of parental permission for someone fourteen years and older."[10]

However, as Father Easton points out, the context of the law as well as pastoral issues must be considered:

Perhaps the Church had a reason for not expressing a maximum age for the requirement of parental permission in this situation other than by reliance on the canonical age of adulthood (eighteen). Most persons fourteen years old are still under the control (albeit, waning) of a parent or guardian. Civil law in most countries would hold such persons accountable in some measure for the care of and actions of such minors. In practice, it would be a fruitless and likely pastorally harmful exercise to receive such a minor into the Church only to find that he or she is prevented from the exercise of the Catholic faith by parents/guardians who are opposed.

Although parental permission for initiation does not appear to be an absolute requirement for one who is over the age of fourteen, pastoral prudence dictates that permission be obtained for those who are fourteen to eighteen years of age. The history, circumstances and family life of the minor must be considered when making a determination whether or not to initiate a person over the age of fourteen who does not have parental permission for admission into the Church. Further, a lack of parental permission should be considered early in the initiation process and not immediately prior to reception of the sacraments.

Finally, Father Easton concludes, "since the law does not expressly state an answer to the question, it is my conclusion that the Church does not forbid continuing to require the consent of parents after the person has reached the fourteenth year of age. The Church appears to leave the matter open to pastoral discretion." Father Easton further believes that obtaining parental permission is always the best option and, that when a minor's family is hostile to initiation, the minor should not be admitted to the initiation process, as the "neophyte could not practice the faith."[11]

I believe that there are special circumstances when a person fourteen to eighteen years of age could be initiated without parental permission, for instance, when the person of that age feels strongly about initiation or if the person is somewhat independent of his or her parents.

To summarize, children who have the use of reason and are of catechetical age are those between the approximate ages of seven and fourteen years. These children follow the first section of Part II of the Rite ("Christian Initiation of Children Who Have Reached Catechetical Age").

However, some children younger than age seven may also have the use of reason and be of catechetical age. These children would also follow the first section of Part II of the Rite. Adolescents who have completed the fourteenth year do not absolutely have to have parental permission for initiation. Persons fourteen years of age and older may follow Part I of the Rite ("Christian Initiation of Adults").

Canonically, persons between the ages of fourteen and eighteen do not need parental permission for initiation. Pastorally, some adolescents between the ages of fourteen and eighteen are still very connected to their family and therefore may follow the first section of Part II of the Rite, particularly if there are other children in the family also being initiated. In all cases, a discernment process is necessary to determine whether or not the child follows the first section of Part II of the Rite.

Why Children Seek Initiation

Understanding why a child is seeking initiation will help determine what type of initiation process is best for the child and the family. The children who come seeking

initiation are unbaptized, baptized, uncatechized, catechized. They are members of Christian families, Catholic families, unchurched families. Their parents are catechumens, Catholics, Baptists, Jews, agnostics. Their reasons for seeking initiation are many.

The Child's Desire

The child's personal desire for initiation is one reason a child may come to the Church. Like Stephen Owens, the child may express a desire "to become Catholic" or "to be baptized." Other children may express their desire in terms of wanting to "learn more about God." Some may say that they want to start "going to church." Others may express themselves in the form of questions. They may begin asking about God or Jesus. They may ask about Baptism, Church, heaven or hell, Scripture or people who are Christians.

Often the child's desire develops as the result of relationships with other Catholic children or adults. The child may attend Catholic school or have friends or neighbors who are Catholic. Other children may have been influenced by a relationship with an adult, such as a relative, teacher, coach, leader or friend. At times, the reason for wanting to join the Church may be unidentifiable. Nonetheless, a child's interests and desires can be as sincere and as serious as an adult's. The source of the desire is explored in a pastoral interview and attended to throughout the entire process.

There are times, however, when a child's desire to be baptized may be questionable. A child may express a desire to "become Catholic" because she or he wants to "fit" and be "like the others" in a class or a group. Peer pressure might be an issue. The desire to belong may be real for the young person, even though it may not be God-focused. This type of longing should be attended to seriously. The child may start the process of initiation, but later stop the journey if his or her intentions are not sincere. The initial reason for seeking initiation may change if the child's participation becomes a journey of conversion. Whatever the reason for the child's desire for initiation, the child should be taken seriously, and discernment regarding ultimate initiation can be made along the way.

The Parent's or Guardian's Desire

A child may have little or no interest in Jesus Christ or the Church when she or he initially makes contact with the Church. Instead, the parent or guardian may be the motivating force behind an inquiry into the Catholic faith. Often, for a child in this situation, the parents are Catholic adults who have been away from church for a number of years. Because they have been away, their children have not been fully initiated. Or, the parents may be inquiring into the faith for themselves, and they bring their children with them. Other times, a guardian or relative brings a child because they feel a child who has not been initiated "needs to be baptized and receive First Communion."

A parent or guardian bringing a child for initiation is a perfectly legitimate way for a child to begin inquiring about the faith. Parents most often know what is best for their child and make decisions for them everyday. Even if a child has no interest or desire initially, once the journey is begun the child may indeed enter into a process of conversion.

If a child is reluctant or resistant, a compromise may have to be negotiated.

Matt, an inquirer in the seventh grade, did not want to participate in the initiation process. His mother was "making" him come.

His mother and the initiation coordinator asked Matt to compromise. Matt agreed to come to the precatechumenate family sessions for three months and then decide if he wanted to continue. After three months, Matt found that he enjoyed the sessions and wanted to continue.

If, however, Matt had continued to resist, the coordinator and parents would have to reconsider the child's readiness for conversion and initiation.

Grandparents', Godparents' or a Relative's Initiative

Corrine was concerned because her eight-year-old granddaughter, Rachel, had not received First Communion and had not been baptized. Her son and daughter-in-law were indifferent about such matters. Rachel was neutral herself, but thought that if Baptism was important to Grandma, then it must be OK. Upon Grandma's insistence, Rachel's parents agreed that Grandma could take Rachel to the parish and ask for her to be "baptized and receive First Communion."

After calling the parish to find out how she could "get her granddaughter baptized," Corrine was asked if she, Rachel and Rachel's parents could meet with the initiation coordinator for an initial interview. Rachel's father reluctantly agreed and together the decision was made that Rachel and her grandma would begin the initiation process.

Grandparents, godparents or relatives bringing a child for initiation is also completely legitimate if the parent is unwilling or unable to bring the child and if the child is agreeable. Usually, parents have agreed in advance to a grandparent's or godparent's bringing a child for full sacramental initiation. Parental permission is important, however, if someone other than the parent is presenting the child for initiation. As long as those presenting the child are willing to support and nurture the child's faith, their commitment to the child is welcome.

A Combination of Reasons

Children and families come forward seeking initiation for many reasons. Sometimes the reasons are singular and clear: a child's desire, a remarriage, a return to church, a friend's invitation. Most often, however, several factors contribute to the decision to seek initiation. What is most important is that the pastoral minister who meets with the family be welcoming, nonjudgmental and open to the complexity of individual situations and the family's history. Understanding the child's family system will help the parish be more effective in its ministry to the child and family. Likewise, understanding why a child has come to the church will help the parish design a process that is best suited for the child.

The Children Who Seek Initiation

Unbaptized Children

Those who have received faith formation or religious instruction. Stephen Owens is one example of an unbaptized child seeking initiation who had received religious instruction and had also been somewhat formed in faith before he began the initiation process.

The depth and type of faith formation or religious instruction the child has had needs to be explored because this will influence the formation process. A child may have received religious instruction from parents, godparents, grandparents, in a Catholic school or catechetical program. That instruction may have been in the Roman or Eastern Catholic tradition, or in the Orthodox, Protestant or Anglican/Episcopalian traditions or in a non-Christian tradition. The initial interview is a helpful first step for determining the type of faith formation a child has had.

In any of the situations just described, the children who are unbaptized and are of catechetical age would ordinarily follow the general pattern of initiation as described in the first section of Part II of the Rite. "Their initiation is to be extended over several years, if need be, before they receive the sacraments of initiation" (#253). And the period of the catechumenate "should extend for at least one year of formation, instruction and probation" (National Statute 6).

The depth and length of the initiation process depends on the needs of the child and the family. The child may know religious facts and doctrine, but may have little understanding of Scripture. Furthermore, the child who knows religious facts may not necessarily have a personal relationship with God.

A major part of one's faith formation includes formation in the community's way of life and worship. Therefore, a child's initiation must also include incorporation into the community. This is especially significant when a child comes to initiation through a Catholic school. Though the child may be a part of the school community, the school does not include the whole parish community and the child must be initiated into the larger parish community. It is when the parish gathers as an assembly for Sunday Eucharist that the Body of Christ is most perfectly manifest. A child's conversion includes incorporation into the community and the paschal mystery.

Those who have not received faith formation or religious instruction. Stacy and Michael Stipes, who were introduced in the first chapter, are examples of unbaptized children who received little formation in faith because their mother had not been practicing her Catholicism. They had some experience with church because of the influence of their grandparents and relatives. They also had some ideas about God and Jesus Christ because of the influence of their mother and other relatives.

Many unbaptized children have no experience of church, and often family members are also unchurched. Even in this type of situation, the child may have some notion of God, because children have an innate sense of the holy and many are aware of God even though they have not received formal instructions in religion. Usually, by the time a child comes to the parish interested in initiation, she or he has some idea of who God is.

Unbaptized children with no previous formation in faith or religious instruction would follow the pattern of initiation as given in the first section of Part II of the Rite. Since they have had little or no faith formation, their initiation could possibly be extended over several years (#253). All the unbaptized children would share in the same process of initiation. They would celebrate the liturgical rites together and share the same formational experiences. However, children with no previous faith formation may have a more extended journey to make. Once again, the needs and history of the children and families will determine the length and requirements of the initiation process.

Baptized Children

Those who have been catechized. Marcus and Marita Addison, along with their father and grandmother, had been active in the First Christian Church. The children had a deep personal relationship with Jesus and a familiarity with Scripture. When their father married a Catholic woman who also had two children, Marcus and Marita began to show interest in the Catholic faith. Two years after the families had been blended, Marcus, Marita and their father expressed a desire to join the Catholic Church.

Like the Addison children, marrying into a Catholic family is one way that baptized, catechized children come to the Catholic Church. When a child's parent marries a Catholic or if a child is adopted into a Catholic family, the child and/or parent(s) may have a desire for the child to become Catholic. Although the children have been baptized and catechized in another tradition, they still have a need to be properly initiated and welcomed into the Catholic Church.

For example, with Marcus and Marita, their background in Scripture was strong but fundamentalist. The lectionary-based catechesis of the catechumenate helped them interpret Scripture more critically and apply its meaning to their lives. Likewise, they each had a strong personal relationship with Jesus Christ that needed to be balanced with the communal dimension of a Christian relationship with God that is so much a part of the Catholic tradition.

In addition, baptized children who have been active in another Christian tradition may decide on their own that they want to become part of the Catholic Church. Though the child's family may not be interested in the Catholic faith, the permission of the parent is required if the child is under fourteen years of age.

In any of these situations, the initiation of a

baptized, catechized child would follow the pattern of initiation as described in the first ("Christian Initiation of Children Who Have Reached Catechetical Age") and fifth ("Reception of Baptized Christians into the Full Communion of the Catholic Church") sections of Part II of the Rite. In other words, the child would need some preparation for initiation (#477, 478) and that might take place with child catechumens. The children who are baptized (candidates) could also celebrate combined rites with the catechumens (see Appendix I of the Rite for combined rites).

The baptism and previous faith formation of the child are to be taken into account when celebrating the rites and designing the formation plan. Some children who are baptized and catechized do not need an extended catechumenate. They need to experience the Catholic Christian community and they may need sacramental catechesis for Confirmation and Eucharist. Baptized, catechized children have different faith formation needs than those who are uncatechized. Those needs and the family situation are to be considered when designing the formation process for each child.

Also, baptized children from other Christian traditions make a profession of faith and are ritually received into the Church. They are to be received into the fullness of the Church with "no greater burden than necessary" (#473). The reception of a baptized child into the full communion of the Catholic Church can take place at any time, but should normally take place within Mass (#475). If the children have been part of a larger group that has journeyed together for some time, they may be received into the Church, and celebrate Confirmation and Eucharist at the Easter Vigil. However, some children may not need a lengthy catechumenal process. Such children can be received into the Church and celebrate Confirmation and Eucharist at a time other than the Vigil.

Lastly, children who are baptized and catechized in the Roman Catholic tradition do not follow the Rite of Christian Initiation of Adults. As children baptized in infancy and catechized in the Roman Catholic tradition, these children celebrate Confirmation and Eucharist according to the guidelines of their local (diocesan) Church. On the other hand, children who were baptized Roman Catholic in infancy, but who have not been catechized, might appropriately follow sections one and four ("Preparation of Uncatechized Adults for Confirmation and Eucharist") of Part II of the Rite.

Those who have not been catechized. Cecilia and Jeffrey Johnson were baptized in the Baptist Church. Although they attended church on occasion, they had received little formation in faith. When Cecilia and Jeff were in junior high school, their mother and stepfather felt that the time was right to return to church. Their stepfather was Catholic, and since he had remained fairly active in his church, the family decided to inquire about the Catholic Church.

Children like Cecilia and Jeff who are baptized but uncatechized would follow the general pattern of initiation in the first and fourth sections of Part II of the Rite. The fourth section pertains to the preparation of baptized but uncatechized adults for Confirmation and Eucharist. The guidelines are given for adults (i.e., those who have attained the use of reason) "who were baptized as infants either as Roman Catholics or as members of another Christian community but did not receive further catechetical formation" (#400). There are many children like Cecilia and Jeff who are baptized but uncatechized. For the most part, the formation of baptized, uncatechized children is similar to the formation of unbaptized, uncatechized children except that the process must recognize that baptized children's "conversion is based on the baptism they have already received, the effects of which they must develop" (#400).

In addition, children baptized in another Christian tradition would make a profession of faith before they are confirmed and receive the Eucharist for the first time—whether that be at the Easter Vigil or at another time.

In other words, children baptized in another Christian community do not just "slide into" the regular religious education program and then receive the sacraments with their baptized Catholic peers. All baptized children, whether catechized or uncatechized need to be properly and fully welcomed into the Catholic Christian community. The length and depth of each child's initiation process depend upon the needs of the child and family.

Those baptized in the Roman Catholic Church. Uncatechized children who were baptized as infants in the Roman Catholic Church could appropriately participate in the process of initiation (#400). They would follow sections one and four of Part II of the Rite. Since the children have been baptized, they would celebrate the liturgical rites for the baptized. Following the same plan of formation as the catechumens follow is often the best option, depending on the age of the children and the circumstances of the family.

In many instances, the needs of baptized, uncatechized Catholic children are similar to children who are unbaptized and uncatechized. In both cases, the children have had little religious formation and little experience with church. In both cases there is a need for conversion. Even though the children were baptized in the Catholic Church, they may need to journey with other children and their families on the path to full sacramental initiation. A thorough pastoral interview will help discern whether involvement in a

catechumenal process is best for the child and family (see #478 on discernment and the length of catechetical formation). Three different scenarios will help describe various options for the baptized Catholic child.

Children whose families have been away from the Church. If the baptized Catholic children and their families have been away from the Church for some time, then often a journey similar to that of catechumens is appropriate. (See #400, 402-409.) The question for discernment is, "Has the child received 'catechetical formation'?" According to paragraph 400 of the Rite, someone baptized as an infant in the Roman Catholic Church who did not "receive further catechetical formation" would follow Part II of the Rite. A helpful way of determining if a child has received catechetical formation is to look at the four elements of a complete catechesis: word, community, worship and service. If a child has received some formation in the word, but has not participated in the life of the Catholic community, its worship and its life of service, then most likely that baptized Catholic would follow Part II of the Rite.

Will is eight years old, and though he was baptized as an infant in the Roman Catholic Church, he has since been away from it. Likewise, his mother has been away from the Church. Will's father is not involved in his life. Will and his mother could participate in a process of initiation similar to that of catechumens because there has been no faith formation and no contact with church since baptism (see #400, 402).

The returning Catholic family participates in the process, though some additional attention is given to the parents who are returning to the Church. And the baptized Catholic children who are candidates for full initiation participate in the liturgical rites that are adapted for their circumstances (#405-407).

Young children whose parents have remained somewhat active in the Church. If the baptized Catholic children are young children (approximately six to eight years old) and if their parents have remained somewhat active in the faith, their needs might best be met by including the children with their peers in the parish's catechetical program. In this case, the child does not need a catechumenal process because the family has stayed somewhat connected to the Church and presumably the child has been informally catechized.

Most parish catechetical programs are broad and inclusive in the primary grades; therefore, a previously uncatechized child could comfortably be included. The child and family may not need a lengthy initiation process if the child has had some faith formation and the family has not been away from the Church too long. In this case, the child would then receive Confirmation and Eucharist along with his or her baptized Catholic peers.

Older children whose parents have remained somewhat active in the Church. A slightly different scenario occurs when a baptized Catholic child is older than six or eight years and has been fairly active in church but "missed" celebrating Confirmation and/or Eucharist with the peer group. In this case, she or he does not need a full process of initiation.

You need to determine if the child has had any faith formation and if his or her faith has been put into practice. A complete catechumenal process is not needed if the child has been formed in faith (either informally or through a parish program) and has participated to some extent in the life of the Church. What may be best for the child is a process of sacramental catechesis that would prepare the child for celebration of Confirmation and/or Eucharist. The Rite of Christian Initiation of Adults is not a "catch

up" program for children who "missed a sacrament."

Some baptized Catholic children do not need catechumenal formation. They may need sacramental catechesis or another type of catechetical formation. Once again, a pastoral interview will help discern the best path for the child. A rigid set of criteria cannot be established ahead of time and in isolation from the individual situations of the child and the family. Each child and family must be considered individually because each has different needs.

Confirmation for the baptized Catholic. For the baptized Catholic, special attention needs to be given to the celebration of the Sacrament of Confirmation. According to the National Statutes, the parish priest does not have the faculty to confirm a baptized Catholic "who without his or her fault never put the faith into practice" (National Statute 28c). "In order to maintain the interrelationship and sequence of Confirmation and Eucharist as defined in canon 842.2, priests who lack the faculty to confirm should seek it from the diocesan bishop, who may, in accord with canon 884.1 grant the faculty if he judges it necessary" (National Statute 29).

In most cases, if the child has journeyed with other children who are being fully initiated at the Easter Vigil, Confirmation by the parish priest at the Vigil would be desirable. However, the permission of the local bishop is necessary.

Catechumens and Candidates

Most parishes will have both unbaptized and baptized children seeking initiation. Although some of their individual needs will be different, the children will benefit from being together in a group for their journey of conversion. Because they share many of the same catechetical and formational needs, a combined process of initiation with catechumens and baptized candidates is appropriate. The significance of a candidate's baptism, however, can never be compromised.

Catechumens and candidates may celebrate combined rites such as those given in Appendix I of the Rite. There are no combined rites given for children, but the rites for adults may be adapted. The rites for children given in section one of Part II can serve as guides for adaptation.

The Parents or Guardians of the Children

The process of initiation of children should be family-centered. Therefore, the hope is that one or both parents or the primary guardian of the child will fully participate in the process. Parents who present their children or who accompany their children in the process come from very different backgrounds. Their experience of the Catholic Church influences the dynamics of the entire group. Being aware of and attentive to the background of the parents is a responsibility of the initiation team.

Frequently, at least one of the parents has been baptized in the Catholic Church. Their own upbringing in the Catholic faith often draws them back. Often, they have been away from the Church and that is why their child of catechetical age has not been fully initiated. Sometimes there is pain and anger associated with their return to the Church. They may have been alienated in some way. Reconciliation may be desired and necessary. When one of the parents is a "returning Catholic," care should be taken to address the

parent's issues and, at the same time, not let negative feelings unduly influence the children's initiation.

Other parents may be "returning Catholics" who are not alienated from the Church. They may have simply drifted away and are now returning. In either case, Catholic parents can be a benefit to the catechumenal group because their history with the Church gives them wonderful Catholic stories to share.

Other parents may come from another religious tradition. These parents may or may not be interested in initiation for themselves. The invitation to them is always extended but never pushed. They, too, are an asset to the catechumenal group because they have stories about their own church, synagogue, temple or mosque and about their relationship with God that can be shared with the children.

Still other parents have had little, if any, involvement in any church. Again, these parents may or may not be inquiring about the Catholic faith. If they do begin the initiation process, unchurched parents can be an asset to the group because they bring their own questions and longings. They may have great questions about searching for God and community. Their stories may include descriptions of growing up without a religious influence. These stories may ring true with children in the group who are experiencing church for the first time.

In any event, as part of the child's family, parents greatly influence their children. Since the initiation of children is a family-centered process, attention must be given to the entire family. The needs and concerns of the parents must be addressed. Understanding the history of the parents is a helpful step in understanding the children.

The Initial Interview

A pastoral interview is an effective and appropriate way to begin to understand a child and her or his family. The interview is a first step in building a relationship. Not only will their reasons for seeking initiation begin to surface but their family story will also provide insight into what is needed along the way as they journey toward initiation.

The initial interview takes place shortly after the child, parent or guardian has made an inquiry. Rather than inviting the family to attend a "first class," or meeting, you should invite the child and parents to come to the parish for a pastoral interview. Or, better yet, you could go to the family's home for the discussion. The purpose of the initial interview is fourfold:

1. to meet the child and her or his family;
2. to discuss their needs, desires and family history;
3. to describe what the Church has to offer;
4. to begin to build a relationship with the family.

You should invite the parent or guardian and the child to meet to discuss the child's initiation. Some people are more comfortable coming to the parish office for a first meeting and others appreciate having the initiation minister come to their home. If there are young children in the family, some parents have difficulty in getting to the parish. A willingness to go to someone's home is a gesture of genuine welcome and outreach. It also provides an opportunity for you to meet the child and family in their home setting and learn something about the culture and background of the family.

Also, meeting the child or children with the parent(s) is helpful. Not only does it afford the opportunity for the parents to give permission for the child to proceed with initiation, it also allows you to see how members of the family interact with each other. A personal interview helps you determine who or what was the impetus for seeking initiation. You might also learn if the child is "being forced" into initiation or if there is reluctance or hesitancy on the part of any of the family members. In addition, you will have the chance to speak to the child as well as the adults. On the other hand, there are some circumstances in which you may meet only with a parent or guardian.

You can begin the discussion by warmly welcoming the child and the parent and by expressing the joy the Church feels because of their interest in the faith. Establishing a welcoming, nonthreatening atmosphere is important since many of those who are inquiring are new to the Church or have been away for some time.

Once you have set a friendly and hospitable tone, you can proceed to find out why the child has been brought for initiation. Here are examples of discussion starters:

"Tell me why you are interested in the Catholic Church."

"Why do want to have your child baptized?" Or, "Tell me why you want to be baptized."

"Your mom says you want to become a Catholic. How do you feel about that?"

You also need to find out if the child is seeking Baptism or if the child has already been baptized. This information also helps to establish the child's previous history of church. When the parent (or other adult) talks about the child's Baptism or desire for Baptism, the conversation easily leads into a discussion about the family's experience of church. For example, one mother said, "Yes, Jessica was baptized when she was about four years old. We were going to church with my sister then. Somehow we just drifted away, and we've never been back."

At this point, you might ask the child or the parent, "What did you like about your church?" Then, "Why do you want to come back?"

Or, another father said, "No, Matt has not been baptized. We've never really gone to church. It just didn't seem important until now." You might follow up by saying, "Why does church seem important now?"

Once again, questions should be nonjudgmental and nonthreatening. The purpose of the questions is to determine what the child's faith experience has been in order to be able to design an appropriate initiation process. Some children have received a deep personal faith from their family but have had little experience of church. Other children have a great familiarity with Bible verses but little understanding of how the stories relate to God and God's people.

Children also need the opportunity to respond to questions. Their responses may differ from that of their parents. You need to know the child's impressions as well. This is particularly important when you ask questions about God. You may say, "Tell me what you know about God." Or, "Do you know any stories from the Bible?" The child's response is likely to be more forthright and to the point than the parent's "second-hand opinion" about what the child knows about God. On the other hand, some children are too shy or unsure to respond to questions. In this case, the parent may want to respond for the child.

Speaking directly to the child also affords the opportunity for a child to express a personal desire for initiation. When you ask a child, "Why do you want to become Catholic?" or, "Why do you want to be baptized?" the child is encouraged to answer honestly. The child may answer, "Because my dad and mom want me to." Or, "My friend Jenny is Catholic, and I like going to church with her." Or, "I don't know." Or they may say, "I don't want

to, my dad is making me."

This kind of information from children is helpful because it allows you to work with the child's true feelings. I sometimes ask if I can speak to a child alone if I feel a conversation without a parent would be helpful. As described earlier, a compromise may have to be reached if a child is "being forced" into initiation.

In some instances, the interview may reveal that a complete process of initiation is not needed. For example, in one interview, I discovered that eight-year-old Scott was a baptized Roman Catholic and had sporadic moments of religious education. Scott had friends in the parish and felt comfortable getting started in the parish catechetical program. His parents had not been active in church but had occasionally sent Scott for religious education. In this case, Scott and his parents needed some sacramental catechesis and religious education. The interview had revealed that a complete process of initiation was not appropriate for Scott and his family.

Often parents are primarily interested in "when my child can be baptized." Though you need to listen and be respectful of this concern, you also need to move the conversation toward the ultimate goal of initiation: a journey of conversion that leads to a deeper relationship with God. You should tell the family how the community will walk with the child and family as they journey together toward the living God and a celebration of the sacraments of initiation. Some of the elements to be included in part three of the interview are:

■ The fact that the process of initiation is a journey of faith and does not have a specific time frame. Every journey progresses differently. Many factors determine the timing of the celebration of the sacraments of initiation.

25

- The word of God and the liturgy, especially as it is proclaimed and celebrated on Sunday, is the primary way the child will be formed in faith.
- Sessions are family-centered. One or both parents and siblings are asked to participate.
- Liturgical rites, or ceremonies, mark important times in the journey.
- Sponsors journey with the child and family.
- Parents are expected to be involved and participate in the family sessions. If not, a sponsor or sponsoring family will journey with the child.
- The child is fully initiated through the three sacraments of initiation.
- The process is flexible and will be adapted to meet each child's needs.

Although this seems like a great deal to discuss at an initial interview, I have found that the sooner some of these topics are discussed the better. Families want to be informed, and they want to know what the expectations are.

Every effort must be made to make the family feel welcome. A positive first step is to invite the family to spend an hour with a pastoral minister in an initial interview. Usually this is the first time anyone from the Church has come to their home or spent time talking to them about their needs.

Although many initiation coordinators feel they do not have time to interview each family, the time spent with each family is unquestionably time well spent. The personal time spent with the family demonstrates that the Church really does care about them and their child. It helps establish a level of trust between you and the family. Then, when the family comes back for precatechumenate gatherings, they feel as though they know someone and they are not "coming in cold."

You can close the discussion by inviting the child and family to join other children and families who are meeting for precatechumenate sessions at the home of one of the parishioners. Or, if there are no precatechumenate sessions currently under way, you can invite the child and family to begin meeting informally with a sponsoring family. In any case, the parish should be ready to welcome children whenever they come. It is unconscionable to tell any inquirers that they will have to wait until September (or whenever) when "classes" begin.

For a sample interview aid, see the appendix, pages 127-133.

Sponsors and Sponsoring Families

The initial interview is a good time to describe the sponsor's role to the inquiring family. A sponsor is a person who "accompanies any candidate seeking admission as a catechumen" (#10). The sponsor, usually a person from the parish, helps the candidate feel at home and welcome in the parish, guides the candidate through the initiation process and responds to the concerns and needs of the child and family. The sponsor also presents the candidate at the liturgical rites and stands as witness "to the candidates' moral character, faith, and intention" (#10). The primary role of the sponsor is to listen, support, pray for and assist the candidate; the sponsor is not expected to be a catechist (much less a theologian!).

The Rite sees the parent or guardian as the primary sponsor for a child. That is, the parent accompanies the child on the journey and presents the child at the liturgical rites. When the parents or guardians are not able to fulfill this role, then their place is to be taken by a sponsor (#260).

However, because many of the parents are new or returning to the Church themselves, they need a sponsor as much as their children do. I believe that it is ideal to recruit parish families to sponsor not only the child but the candidate's entire family as well. In this way, the child has a sponsor who is an active, practicing Catholic and the candidate's parents also receive support from another family. Likewise, if the sponsoring family and the candidate's family have children of similar ages, then the children who are candidates for initiation have the opportunity to interact with baptized peers. When children are involved as part of a sponsoring family, the message is given that children are important and that they play an active role in the Church.

Even though families are excellent sponsors for children seeking initiation, individuals may also be sponsors. Teens (at least sixteen years of age) may sponsor other teens, or teens may sponsor younger children.[12] Once again, this is a good way to involve young people and give them responsibility. Because being a sponsor is a great responsibility, however, a sponsoring teen's parents need to be consulted and need to be aware of the responsibility that the teen is undertaking. If possible, the teen's family could also be involved in the process as a sponsoring family, as ministers of hospitality or in some other way.

Individual adults or couples can also sponsor a child. Seniors who love children make excellent sponsors, particularly for children whose grandparents are not living or do not live nearby. Young adults and young couples who do not have children of their own also make good sponsors.

When recruiting sponsoring families, look for families who have a sense of hospitality, compassion and openness and a willingness to share their own story.

Although sponsoring families need to be those who feel at home in the parish so they can help others feel at home, sometimes quiet, "uninvolved" families make the best sponsors. And, being a sponsoring family helps the "uninvolved family" feel more attached to the heart of the parish. The initiation process can become a journey of continuing conversion for the sponsoring family, too.

When recruiting individuals or couples as sponsors, look for people who enjoy spending time with children, who can easily talk to children and who want to listen to them. Persons who do not have the skill or desire to be catechists but who delight in children are potential sponsors.

All children's sponsors need to undergo formation similar to that for adult sponsors. Topics such as the responsibilities, qualities and skills of a sponsor are addressed in sponsor formation. For more on sponsor formation see materials such as *Finding and Forming Sponsors and Godparents*, James Wilde, ed. (Paulist Press); *Guide for Sponsors*, 3rd edition, Ronald Lewinski (Liturgy Training Publications); *Walking Together in Faith: A Workbook for Sponsors in Christian Initiation*, Thomas Morris (Paulist Press).

You should provide sponsors with background in children's spirituality (see Chapter Three). Sponsors also need to understand how to be supportive of a child and her or his family. If there are special circumstances in a candidate's family, a sponsor may need to know that. Sponsors need information and ideas on ways to interact with a catechumenal family. Encourage sponsoring families to invite their candidates to their homes, to parish events and to other outside activities. Each family pair (catechumenal family and sponsoring family) will have a different pattern of interaction. Some people are naturally comfortable interacting as sponsors, and others need more encouragement from you or a sponsor coordinator. Whatever the circumstances of the candidate and sponsor, what is most important is that they spend some quality time together.

Lastly, there is a difference between sponsors and godparents. The godparent may be a person other than the parish sponsor. The godparent is chosen by the child and family. The godparent may be a relative or friend who lives elsewhere. The godparent presents the child at the Rite of Election and at the celebration of the sacraments of initiation. Even though the godparents may be present for the rites, a parish sponsor is still an important connection with the local community. Some children may have parish sponsors and godparents. For others, the parish sponsor and the godparent may be the same person (see General Introduction, #8-10 and *Rite*, Introduction, #9-10).

Special Situations in the Family

Uninvolved Parents

Although one hopes that the candidate's parent(s) will be actively involved in the child's journey of conversion, there are times when the parent(s) cannot sponsor the child through the parish process of initiation. Many parents are under an inordinate amount of stress, and sometimes life is simply too complicated for a parent to make a commitment to a weekly initiation gathering.

June, a single mother at St. Anthony Parish, is rearing five children and two grandchildren. She also works a night job. The family attends church only on an occasional basis. The three youngest children have requested Baptism. Although June supports their desire to be baptized, she finds it impossible to make a commitment to bring them to weekly precatechumenate sessions. She cannot even

make a commitment to bringing them to church.

A parent's inability to participate in the initiation process, is not, in and of itself, an adequate reason to deny sacramental initiation to a child. A sponsor or sponsoring family can walk with the child through the process of initiation. In this instance, the James family, who had children of similar ages, sponsored June's children on their journey. Margaret James brought the children to and from the sessions and also took them to and from church. This continued for two years until June's life settled down enough that she could come to church with her children.

In other families, the parent(s) may have the ability to participate, but they may lack the desire or commitment to be involved.

Thirteen-year-old Kristin wants to become Catholic, but no one else in her family has any interest in the Catholic Church or in actively living the life of a worshiping Christian. At the initial interview, Kristin and her father discussed this situation with the initiation coordinator. Kristin's father gave his permission for Kristin to participate in the process and be sacramentally initiated, but neither he nor Kristin's mother wanted to be involved.

This is a serious situation because children "are dependent on their parents or guardians" (#252). How can a child grow in faith if there is no support in the home? On the other hand, the child has attained the use of reason, has parental permission and has a desire for initiation. Is lack of parental support in this instance an adequate reason to deny initiation?

Some may argue that without support in the home, a living faith cannot develop and flourish. No one will bring the child to church or nurture her or his faith after initiation. Once again, a sponsor or sponsoring family can provide the necessary support and guidance. And, a child may seek Christian initiation, "with parental permission, on their own initiative" (#252). Therefore, lack of parental involvement is not sufficient reason to deny sacramental initiation to a child.

In the case of thirteen-year-old Kristin, a "sixty-something" couple from the parish agreed to sponsor her. Their granddaughter was a friend of Kristin's, and they appreciated the opportunity to help Kristin and to spend time with their granddaughter as well. They attended all of the sessions with Kristin, as did their granddaughter. They stood up with her at all of the rites. After initiation, they continued to bring her to church and to other formational sessions for teens.

If you think that finding sponsors to commit to such a great responsibility is not possible, let me assure you that it can be done. Finding the right people to sponsor children certainly takes a great deal of time and effort, but the young inquirers deserve no less than your best effort. And, when the right people are asked to sponsor a child, the experience most often proves to be a lasting, rewarding, faith-enriching relationship for all involved.

Children of Various Ages

Within a family, the age range of children to be initiated may be great. This can present a challenge during the formation process as well as at the time of sacramental initiation.

The Walker family, an inquiring family at St. Patrick Parish, has three children: Erica, age thirteen; Nick, age nine; and Courtney, age four. In addition, the father, David, is also inquiring. The mother, Monica, is an inactive Catholic. At the time the Walkers began the precatechumenate, two children already involved in the process at St. Patrick were age seven. The parish wondered how to coordinate suitable pastoral formation for such a wide-ranging age group and secondly, if the four-

year-old child should be fully initiated with the rest of the family.

Here's how we handled this situation.

First, family sessions, which are intergenerational, involve people of all ages and thus diminish the differences in ages among the children. When sponsors and sponsoring families are added, the age difference is diminished even further. In the case of the Walker family and St. Patrick Parish, the intergenerational sessions included the Walkers, their sponsoring family, the two other seven-year-old inquiring children and their sponsoring families. Thirteen-year-old Erica had a companion from her sponsoring family and the other children in the group were close enough in age that nine-year-old Nick felt comfortable as well.

A second concern regarding various ages within a single family arises when one of the children is younger than seven. At the present time, there are two paths to initiation. For those who have not attained the use of reason, the path includes Baptism, with Confirmation and Eucharist delayed. For those who have reached the age of reason, the path culminates with Baptism, Confirmation and Eucharist, usually celebrated at the Easter Vigil. Therefore, a family like the Walkers would have two children who would be fully initiated at the Vigil and one child who would not. The inconsistency of the Church's practice makes this is a difficult situation.

In some instances, the situation resolves itself. If a child is five or six years old when she or he begins the process of initiation, by the time the sacraments are celebrated the child may be seven years of age (the age of reason). What is most important is that the child has exhibited an ability to receive and nurture a personal faith (#252). Yet again, some children who are four, five or six years old may have already "attained the use of reason" and are therefore no longer considered infants.

29

If they, too, have exhibited an ability to receive and nurture a personal faith, they would be fully initiated with the rest of the family at the Easter Vigil.

Great priority should be given to keeping the family together throughout the entire journey of initiation.

A Single Child or Family

The parish has a responsibility of always being ready to welcome anyone who approaches it seeking possible membership. This is true whether the parish routinely welcomes fifty or a hundred inquirers a year or whether there is only a single child or a single family seeking initiation. The family should not be made to wait until more inquirers appear. Nor should they have to "wait until September" when the parish is ready again. Instead, the child and family could be paired with a sponsoring family. Depending on the circumstances, the sponsoring family might also be asked to serve as catechists for the child. Although the hope is that there will be enough children to form a catechumenal group, this may not always be the case. Instead, there may just be the catechumen's family and the sponsor's family journeying together within the community of the faithful. You need to work closely with the families, providing support, materials and guidance.

The Community: Parish, Family, Companions

The parish community influences the inquiring children in many ways. In general, through evangelization, catechesis, social activities, works of apostolic service and worship, the Christian community forms and supports its inquirers. More specifically, however, children experience community through their families and through their peers. "The children's progress in the formation they receive depends on the help and example of their companions and on the influence of their parents" (#254). Let's take a look now at the role of the companion.

Companions of the children are those "of the same age who are already baptized and are preparing for confirmation and Eucharist." Furthermore, the candidates' initiation "progresses gradually and within the supportive setting of this group of companions" (#254.1) The Rite says "it is advantageous, as circumstances allow, to form a group of several children who are in this same situation, in order that by example they may help one another in their progress as catechumens" (#255). In other words, the Rite envisions the candidates as part of a catechumenal group, yet also involved with their baptized peers.

There are several ways you can make this dynamic happen. First, regularly gather the group of children who are inquirers, catechumens or candidates for precatechumenate and catechumenate sessions with their families. During the catechumenate, gather them each Sunday for the Liturgy of the Word and the breaking open of the word. In this way, the children are with others "who are in the same situation."

The candidates' companions are children from the parish who support the candidates along the way. They are generally close in age to the candidates. They might be friends or acquaintances from school or the neighborhood who are members of the parish. Companions may occasionally, or on a regular basis, participate in precatechumenate and catechumenate session. A companion might also be a member of a sponsoring family. Since sponsoring families participate in the intergenerational sessions, catechumens and candidates receive "help" from these baptized companions who are members of the sponsoring families. When sponsoring families spend time with a candidate, the candidate can easily interact with her or his baptized peer.

Another way for the children's initiation to progress "gradually and within the supportive setting of this group of companions" is for the candidates to participate in some of their peers' activities. Although some catechetical activities are not appropriate for inquirers or catechumens, other activities lend themselves nicely to participation by the baptized as well as the candidates. For example, when the junior high youth at St. Perpetua Parish gathered to make Easter baskets for needy families, the junior high candidates joined them for the work and for the soup-and-bread supper that followed. Junior high and high school candidates might also participate in some of the social activities of their peers. The candidates are most comfortable doing this when their sponsors or friends are involved. Asking an adolescent to come "solo" to a parish youth gathering might be intimidating.

Similarly, seven- and eight-year-old catechumens at St. Perpetua joined their baptized peers for Saturday morning sacramental catechesis. Baptized children preparing for First Eucharist met with their parents on Saturday mornings. Catechumens, along with their parents, also participated in these sessions, which focused on the symbols of the Eucharist. Since all the children were preparing for Eucharist, the sessions were appropriate for the baptized as well as the catechumens. There may be times when sacramental catechesis for baptized confirmation candidates could be shared with catechumens. In fact, National Statute 19 refers to "the catechetical instruction of baptized children before their celebration of the sacraments" being shared with catechumens.

Candidates and catechumens in a Catholic school also benefit from the example of their classmates and peers. Companions in the Catholic school provide support for the candidates and catechumens through their everyday activities. In addition to daily interaction, schoolmates may celebrate some of the minor rites of the catechumenate with the candidates (#85-103). Celebrations of the word, blessings, anointing and exorcisms are easily celebrated in the Catholic school setting. These celebrations benefit not only the candidates and catechumens but also the baptized companions, particularly those who may not regularly worship on Sunday with the candidates. Celebrations in the school allow for the Catholic school peers to pray for the candidates in a liturgical context. Since their classmates are part of their Christian community, celebrations with the Catholic school community allow for the candidates' "entire community" to be involved in their formation (#80).

Relationship to Catechetical Program, Catholic School and Youth Ministry

Candidates for full initiation interact and form communion with their baptized companions in the catechetical group, in the Catholic school and in youth ministry. Even though there is a relationship among the children of the various groups, the process of initiation is distinct from any parish catechetical program. In other words, the process of initiation for children of catechetical age is not a catechetical program, nor, in the case of adolescents, is it a youth ministry program. The initiation of children of catechetical age belongs to the liturgical order found in the Rite of Christian Initiation of Adults.

Child catechumens and candidates, then, journey through the process of initiation with the full support of their baptized companions; after full initiation, they participate in the catechetical program for the baptized. In general, catechesis for baptized children is not appropriate for catechumens. Also, to ask a child and family to participate in a parish catechetical program and a process of initiation is too taxing and time-consuming for any family.

If a child has a great desire to participate in a parish catechetical program because friends or peers are involved, exceptions can be made. I ask the child and family if they would like to participate in both the catechumenal process and the catechetical program. However, the children's "condition and status as catechumens" cannot be "compromised or confused, nor should they receive the sacraments of initiation in any sequence other than that determined in the ritual of Christian initiation" (National Statute 19).

Each parish situation and each catechetical program is different. Many people from small parishes have told me that they have had great success with including candidates into their catechetical program. In some cases, catechetical classes are small enough and flexible enough to adapt to the needs of a catechumen or candidate. Likewise, if your catechetical program is lectionary-based, it might easily be adapted to include candidates who have entered the period of the catechumenate.

The Christian Initiation Team

In addition to the parish at large, the sponsors and the companions, the Christian initiation team plays an important role in the initiation of children. The initiation team coordinates the details of the parish process of initiation for both children and adults. One team guides the way the parish welcomes those seeking initiation. Just as there is one process of initiation, there is one team to facilitate that process. However, some of the team members may work specifically with adults or specifically with children

Every parish has its own unique initiation team. Every team is different because every parish is different and has its own needs and ways of functioning. Here is one model for an initiation team. A similar model was used in a fairly large (1,000 families) suburban, middle-class parish without a Catholic school. Approximately six to ten children of catechetical age were involved in initiation at any given time.

Team Members

- Director of Christian Initiation—Directs the overall process of initiation for adults and children.
- Coordinator of Children's Initiation—Coordinates the process for the children and their families, interviews children and families, recruits and trains catechists for children.
- Liturgist—Responsible for the preparation and celebration of the rites.
- Priest—Presides at rites and serves as a catechist.
- Coordinator of Sponsors—Recruits and trains sponsors and sponsoring families for children; recruits and trains sponsors for adults.
- Coordinator of Hospitality—Prepares hospitality and environment for sessions for children and adults; prepares receptions after the rites.
- Catechists—Carry out varying roles and responsibilities depending upon the

individual's time, gifts and skills.

- Precatechumenate Catechist for Children—Facilitates precatechumenate sessions for inquiring children and their families. Children and adults may have combined sessions at times.
- Precatechumenate Catechist for Adults—Facilitates precatechumenate sessions for inquiring adults. Children and adults may have combined sessions at times.
- Catechumenate Catechist for Children—Facilitates breaking open the word and the extended catechesis that follows. One catechist may do breaking open the word and another may do the extended catechesis or the same person may do both. Catechists may also lead sessions during the periods of purification and enlightenment and mystagogy.
- Catechumenate Catechist for Adults—Facilitates breaking open the word and the extended catechesis that follows. One catechist may do breaking open the word and another may do the extended catechesis or the same person may do both. Catechists may also lead sessions during the periods of purification and enlightenment and mystagogy.
- Mystagogue—Facilitates reflection on sacramental initiation and helps neophytes deepen their grasp of the paschal mystery.

Other roles are possible. For example, there could be spiritual directors who work with inquirers, catechumens and candidates to help them discern conversion and readiness for initiation. Each parish develops the team that best fits the process for that parish. Developing a complete team may take a number of months or years. Finding the right people and training them do their job well takes time and effort.

Summary

The entire parish is needed in order for the process of initiation to be full, rich and satisfying. The initiation team, the sponsoring families and sponsors and companions have a particularly important role. The uniqueness of each child and each family makes the ministry of initiation a privilege and sometimes a challenge. Every child and every family has a different story and a different journey. Therefore, each must be given careful, loving and individual attention. Even though each journey is unique, the children and the faithful walk the path together.

REFERENCES

1 James A. Coriden, Thomas J. Green and Donald E. Heintschel, *The Code of Canon Law: A Text and Commentary* (New York: Paulist Press, 1985), pp. 31-32.

2 Ibid., p. 32.

3 Emily Filippi, a team member of the North American Forum on the Catechumenate, pointed this out to me during a discussion, 8 May 1996.

4 A discussion with team members from the North American Forum on the Catechumenate, 8 May 1996, highlighted for me the significance of the "and" in this statement.

5 Consultation with Rev. Frederick C. Easton, J.C.L., Vicar Judicial, Archdiocese of Indianapolis, 11 April 1996.

6 John M. Huels, *The Catechumenate and the Law: A Pastoral and Canonical Commentary for the Church in the United States* (Chicago: Liturgy Training Publications, 1994), p. 25.

7 It says, "The baptism of adults, at least those who have completed fourteen years of age is to be referred to the bishop so that it may be conferred by him, if he judges it expedient."

8 Easton.

9 Huels, p. 25.

10 Easton.

11 Ibid.

12 *Code of Canon Law*, canon 874, p. 629.

3

The Period of Evangelization and Precatechumenate

"Why are God and the devil always a man and never a woman?" *Marty, age eleven*

"Do I have to be baptized to get to heaven?" *Erica, age thirteen*

"My uncle out in Oregon is really sick. We think he's going to die." *Michael, age eight*

"Is the Holy Spirit God?" *Joe, age seven*

"My brother embarrasses me. It makes me angry." *Mariah, age eight (Her brother had severe learning disabilities.)*

These are some of the thoughts and questions that children ask during the period of evangelization and precatechumenate. This first period of the initiation process is a time of evangelization when "faithfully and constantly the living God is proclaimed and Jesus Christ whom he has sent for the salvation of all" (#36).

The living God is proclaimed to children and their families through storytelling. The children tell their stories and connect those stories to the great stories of God and God's people. Through the sharing of stories, the children come to know better our loving God. In turn, the sharing of stories leads children to ask the questions burning deeply in their hearts. The key to evangelization is storytelling and asking questions.

In Pope Paul VI's apostolic exhortation *Evangelii nuntiandi* ("Evangelization in the Modern World"), the pope describes evangelization as "proclaiming Christ to those who do not know Him."[1] Storytelling is one highly effective way to proclaim Christ to children. Everyone loves stories, and children are particularly captivated by them. Scripture stories speak to children about the Good News of Jesus Christ. The Christmas story and the stories of the "lost" boy (the Child Jesus in the Temple), of the short man in the tree (Zacchaeus), of the lost pet (sheep) and of the lost allowance (the coin), of the calming of the terrifying thunderstorm, of Jesus' bringing a little girl back to life, and countless others appeal to children and help them to come to know Jesus Christ and his mission.

Pope Paul also pointed out that "evangelizing means bringing the Good News into all the strata of humanity, and through its influence transforming humanity from within and making it new...."[2] For children, this means that the Good News has transforming power for their lives at home and school, in the neighborhood, at daycare, the mall, work, ball practice, dance class, the playground and Grandma's. The Good News transforms the entire strata of their young lives.

Likewise, Pope John Paul II emphasizes the transforming power of the Good News when he says that evangelization is a "personal and profound meeting" with Jesus Christ that leads to conversion.[3] Generally, children are eager to know Jesus. They are much more open to getting to know the person of Jesus Christ than they are to learning about Catholic doctrine. Evangelization is a time for coming to know Jesus Christ through the sharing of the Christian stories: Scripture stories, parish stories, stories of saints and sinners, stories of tradition and personal stories. As the child comes to know Jesus, conversion begins.

Evangelizing Children

Evangelization happens in telling and listening to stories. Children have rich, delightful and serious stories to tell. They also have deep, insightful questions to ask. Listening to their stories, telling our stories, responding to their questions, asking more questions and addressing their concerns is at the heart of evangelization for children. Children approach the Church with a natural sense of awe and wonder. They are eager to explore the life of the Holy One they cannot see. The period of evangelization and precatechumenate is a time to open up already receptive hearts and minds to the wondrous workings of the living God.

Children's Spirituality

Although some pastoral ministers believe that children do not have enough experience in life to ask the big questions, most parents, child psychologists and religious educators know that children have a innate spirituality that makes them ripe for evangelization.

In his book *The Spiritual Life of Children*, Robert Coles has documented discussions, insights, questions, stories and artwork from children that illustrate their profound sense of connectedness to the holy. Coles gives accounts of his interviews with children that portray a remarkable spiritual depth. Also, the interviews highlight some of the "eternal questions children ask more intensely, unremittingly and subtly than we sometimes imagine."[4] Coles's work points to the fact that children do indeed have a sense of God's presence in their lives. Children intuitively know that their lives are intertwined with the Divine. As one nine-year-old girl put it, God is the "companion who won't leave."[5]

Since not all children may be able to articulate their sense of the Holy, Coles cautions that a great deal of time needs to be spent with a child before she or he may feel confident and comfortable enough to express her or his innermost feelings about God. Coles says that often "months or years" are needed "to learn of a child's sense of spiritual connectedness and continuity."[6]

This is not to say that months will pass before a child will share his or her thoughts and feelings about the Divine. Rather, the point is that children need time to build trusting relationships. The process of evangelization cannot be rushed or put into a rigid time frame. On the other hand, a child may feel or have a "spiritual connectedness" without verbally expressing it. Some children are very quiet and reserved and may not want to publicly articulate their sense of God. The skilled initiation catechist can use other methods to evangelize the child. Like Coles, the catechist may invite the child to express ideas about God and self through drawing or painting. The catechist might also use sculpture, music or movement and dance as a way of inviting the child to share her or his story.

Children's Stories and Questions

Since evangelization happens through storytelling, children should be invited to share their stories and then to see the connection between their story and God's story as found in the Scriptures, in the tradition and in life. As they make the connections between their story and God's story, they then begin to ask questions about how and why this God makes a difference in their lives.

In one precatechumenate session, the inquiring children and their families were talking about their images of God. As Marty's mother was talking about her image of God, Marty blurted out, "Why are God and the devil always a man and never a woman?"

The catechist asked, "What do you think, Marty?"

Although Marty said he wasn't sure why, he had noticed that in the Bible and in books and pictures God was always a man. What followed was a lively discussion among the parents and children regarding the nature of the Divine.

Furthermore, the catechist made note of Marty's question and later began to realize its depth. In an earlier session, Marty had talked about his family. He had been born in Peru and reared primarily by his mother. His family had moved around a great deal. His mother was his main source of security and stability, and she had recently married and was expecting a child. Marty often spoke about his mother and the unborn baby.

The perceptive catechist saw that Marty's image of God was grounded in the close relationship he had with his mother. The catechist built on the maternal image of God and helped Marty make the connection between his experience of his mother's strong, steadfast love and the strong, steadfast love of God. Furthermore, Scripture stories about creation, Wisdom, Sarah, Hagar, Elizabeth and Mary enhanced Marty's understanding and experience of God. Likewise, the entire group benefited from Marty's question and from the follow-through of the catechist.

Children frequently ask questions like the one Marty asked. Catechists need to pick up on those questions and look behind what is being asked. Often children's concerns, fears, hopes and dreams are expressed in their questions and comments. The skilled catechist will gently lead the child to see how God is in the midst of all.

In addition to responding to the initial questions, the catechist must encourage the child to ask deeper questions. In Marty's case, the catechist helped him see God in new and different ways and encouraged him to ask other questions: "Does God love everybody? Even terrorists, like the Oklahoma City bomber?"

Sharing stories and asking questions, then, is the key to evangelizing children. Children are invited to share their stories and to listen to the stories of the Christian community and to ask questions about God, themselves and life. Through the exchange of stories and questions, children hear and take to heart the Good News of Jesus Christ and of the living God.

Evangelizing the Family

The entire family must be considered in order to fully evangelize the child. Proclaiming the living God to children includes helping children see how God is already active and present in their families, where their lives are centered. Evangelization is much more effective when it is directed to the entire family.

Evangelizing the family is much the same

as evangelizing the child. Families are invited to share their stories and make the connections between their family and God's family. This allows family members to witness to one another about how and where they see God working in their home. Children are intrigued when they hear their parents talk about God's presence in their lives, and they are often quite impressed when they hear a parent tell the story of how God was present when they were born. Likewise, parents usually are surprised at the depth and insights their children have. Many parents have not heard their children speak much about God or about God working in their lives. Often the period of evangelization and precatechumenate is the first time children and parents have listened to one another tell their stories. So, families learn not only about God and God's story but they also learn about each other.

During a precatechumenate session at Our Lady of Good Counsel Parish, the group was discussing their "family histories" and naming times when they felt God was present in their families.

Daniel was telling the story of how he was born with a hole in his heart and had to have heart surgery when he was a newborn baby. He said he believed God was there with him and his family, because God helped him through the surgery.

Susan, Daniel's mother, also told the same story. She added, however, that Daniel's doctors said there was a chance that Daniel may not live through surgery. Daniel had never heard that part of the story. He was curious to know more and was now convinced that he was special since God helped him live. This, in turn, prompted even more discussion about God and why some people live and others die.

Interestingly, all the children in that particular group had a significant or recent experience of a loved one dying. Daniel's and

Susan's sharing of their family's story opened the way for a meaningful discussion about God's promise of eternal life.

sample session

A Method for Evangelizing During the Period of Evangelization and Precatechumenate

Children and families can be evangelized in any number of ways. Most children and their parents have already heard something of the Good News before they approach the parish. Frequently, they have been initially evangelized by friends, classmates, neighbors, coworkers or relatives. They have heard stories, and they come to the parish because they want to know more.

Once they have approached the parish, evangelization continues informally. Children and adults are evangelized as they interact with parishioners and hear the stories of the parish. On the other hand, during the precatechumenate period, a more systematic approach to evangelization is used. Although evangelization cannot be limited to one moment, process or method, it is greatly facilitated through the sharing of stories at the precatechumenate sessions.

Here is a method for storytelling during the precatechumenate. It is based upon a storytelling process offered by the North American Forum on the Catechumenate at its Beginnings and Beyond Institutes and upon the "Shared Christian Praxis" method of

Thomas Groome. I have successfully used this method in parish precatechumenate sessions with children, their families and sponsoring families. There are four movements to the method:

1. Sharing My Story
2. Sharing God's Story
3. Connecting My Story and God's Story
4. Inviting a Response

A gathering and a closing are also added to the four basic movements.

In order to use this storytelling method for precatechumenate sessions, you must remember that evangelization starts long before the precatechumenate session begins. When designing a precatechumenate session, initiation team members must take into consideration what they already know about the inquiring children's stories. The history and questions of the children and their families set the agenda for the precatechumenate session.

For example, if the initial pastoral interview showed that one or more of the children had little understanding of God, then the early precatechumenate sessions should focus on introducing the children to God. If the initial interview showed that an inquiring child was concerned about "what to do during church," or "Jesus' 'real' dad," then time should be spent on those topics. In other words, listening to the stories of the children before the precatechumenate sessions ever begin is a necessary step. Only after listening does the initiation team decide the shape and content of the first precatechumenate sessions.

The inquirers at St. Patrick Parish were very young (ages five to eight) and uncertain about why they were coming and what they doing. The initial interviews showed that, in general, the children knew of God and Jesus Christ, but they weren't sure why they were coming to "these classes" at church.

In this instance, the precatechumenate team decided that the first session would deal with the Good News of God's invitation to all humankind to become members of God's family.

The team also decided that the call of Abraham and Sarah would be the basis for proclaiming this Good News. The session would invite the children to connect their stories of being called to Abraham and Sarah's story. The session would be about trusting in God and following God's call. The sample session given below is similar to the one designed for St. Patrick Parish's inquirers and families.

■ Gathering and Introduction
■ Sharing My Story
■ Sharing God's Story
■ Connecting My Story to God's Story
■ Inviting a Response
■ Closing

Gathering and Introduction

Warmly welcome each child and family by name. Provide plentiful hospitality. Have drinks and snacks available for children and adults. Since the potential exists for new inquirers to be present at any session, plan a simple, fun introductory exercise that will help people learn names and get to know each other.

Catechist: Today we are going to talk about what happens when God invites us on a journey. What is a journey? A journey is a trip, an outing or a visit. To begin, I'd like each person to tell us your name and then answer these two questions:

What is your favorite place to visit? (The library, Grandpa's, McDonald's, the beach...)

If you could go anywhere in the world, where would you go?

Sharing My Story

In this movement, a question, game, current event, movie or activity is used to invite children to share some part of their story. As catechist, you may want to talk about a current event in school, the town or community as a point of departure for children's sharing. Or, you may use a popular movie, song or book as the catalyst.

The children and their families are invited to remember a time when they were asked to go on a trip. They may have been invited by Grandma to go to her house. They may have been asked to go to McDonald's with a friend. They may have been on vacation with their family. They may have been asked to go to the zoo with their classmates. Parents may have been asked to go on a business trip or to a party.

Ask each family member to write down certain details about the trip:

■ Who asked you to go?
■ Where were you asked to go?
■ What did you do to get ready?
■ What feelings did you have about going on the trip?
■ Describe the trip itself, i.e., actually going to the place.
■ How did you feel when you arrived?

Family members work alone at first and then share their responses with each other. Parents help younger children as needed. Next, the inquiring family shares with the sponsoring family.

Sharing God's Story

Now, tell a story from Scripture. The story may be told in storytelling fashion or proclaimed from the Bible. You should then give a simple explanation of the story.

"Tell the story" of God's asking Abraham and Sarah to leave their home and travel to a new land (Genesis 12:1-9ff).

Explanation of the story: God asked Abraham and Sarah to leave their home. This was a very big request! God asked them to leave their home and their country and go to a foreign land where they would not know anyone. Abraham and Sarah had to trust in God and be very courageous to set out on a journey when they didn't know exactly where they were going. God said to go to "the place that I will show you." The story says that Abraham and Sarah "journeyed." That's the word I used earlier, too. In Hebrew, the language that this story was first written down in, the word for *journey* means to pull up tent stakes.[7] The fact that they were pulling up tent stakes means they were moving on for good. They were making a big change. They were not going to be going back. It was a big move!

Connecting My Story to God's Story

In this movement, you need to help the families see connections between their story and God's story.

Now, invite the family pairs (inquiring family and sponsoring family) to discuss the questions given below. Parents should gently encourage children who may be reluctant to share.

■ How do you think Abraham and Sarah felt about leaving their home?
■ Have you ever had to move?
■ How did you feel?
■ How would you feel if you had to move?
■ How is Abraham and Sarah's trip the same or different from the "trip" or outing you described?
■ God was present throughout the journey of Abraham and Sarah. How was God present in your trip?

After adequate discussion time, you should invite the family pairs to share their responses to the last question with the larger group. Then, describe the family's presence at the precatechumenate sessions as their response to God's call. Continue to lead the children to see how God has invited them to begin a journey called "Christian initiation." Here are some points you should cover in the discussion:

- There are many kinds of journeys (cite ones named by the children). Christian initiation is a special kind of journey.
- God calls us to the journey of Christian initiation.
- God asks us to trust like Abraham and Sarah trusted God.
- Time and effort are needed when you are taking a trip or going on an outing or a journey.
- The time and length of the journey are sometimes uncertain.
- There may be times when you doubt or have questions.
- Give pertinent details of the parish initiation process.

Inviting a Response

With a simple question, reflection or challenge, ask the families to look at how the story affects their lives.

Invite the children and their families to respond to the question "Is God's invitation to you Good News? Why or why not?" And, "What questions do you have about Abraham and Sarah's journey or the journey of Christian initiation that you have begun?" In this way, children can ask about a personal concern, or they can express their concerns by asking about Abraham and Sarah.

After the family pairs have discussed the question, the responses are shared in the larger group. Questions that need an extended response can be answered at a later time.

Closing

To close the session, you should lead a simple prayer. A variety of prayer forms can be

introduced at the precatechumenate sessions. The example given below is a framework that was used frequently throughout the precatechumenate at St. Patrick.

- Song
- Reading: Genesis 12:1-4a
- Responsorial Psalm: Psalm 33 (sung) (Note: For a cassette tape of psalms for use with children see Christopher Walker's *Children's Liturgy of the Word*, available from Oregon Catholic Press.)
- Intercessions
- Closing Prayer

Catechesis for the Period of Evangelization and Precatechumenate

Evangelization includes catechesis.[8] Although it is not the only method, or means, of evangelization, catechesis is one of the many ways in which the Good News is echoed. The precatechumenate session described above could be described as catechesis, that is, the word of God was echoed and the developing faith of the inquirers was nourished.

The period of evangelization and precatechumenate includes some catechesis for the children. The content of the catechesis for this period is determined in two ways. First, the stories, needs, desires and questions of the children themselves will determine the content. Secondly, the Rite of Acceptance Into the Order of Catechumens helps determine the catechesis.

Some of the needs, desires and questions of children surface at the pastoral interview. Another way to think about the needs and desires of a child is to consider the general needs and desires of all children. When I meet with parents and catechists, I often ask, "What do children need? What do they deeply desire?" Inevitably, some of the same needs and desires surface: security, fun, friendship, stability, love, discipline, affirmation, a home, acceptance, consistency, family, assurance.

The precatechumenate sessions are designed to address these and similar needs and desires. In other words, the sessions are designed according to the children's agenda, rather than your agenda or what you think might be the Church's agenda.

For children, the constant, steadfast and unending love of God is Good News far more than the any list of apostles' names or the memorization of the works of mercy or number of sacraments. Scripture stories about God's strong, steadfast love reassures children who may be afraid or feel insecure. For example, stories from the exodus event or stories like Daniel and the lions' den speak to children about God's strong and steadfast love.

When you are planning sessions for the children, you must always consider the issues, concerns and needs of the children. Once again, the initiation coordinator and catechists must personally know the children and their families so that sessions are designed according to the children's needs.

The second element that determines the content for the period of precatechumenate is the Rite of Acceptance Into the Order of Catechumens. A careful, reflective, prayerful, in-depth study of the Rite of Acceptance is necessary to see how it affects the period that precedes it. Since the Rite of Acceptance is a culmination of all that has happened before its celebration, you can determine what is to happen during the period of the precatechumenate by studying the rite and more or less working backward.

For example, by looking at the "Outline of the Rite" (found prior to #262), you will see that one of the elements of the rite is the "Signing of the Candidates with the Cross." The cross is a central symbol in the celebration of the rite and its prominence indicates that the importance of the cross would have been included in the period of the precatechumenate. In other words, catechesis about the cross should have taken place in the period of evangelization and precatechumenate.

This is just one example of how the rite helps determine the catechesis for the period of the precatechumenate. Let's take a look at the rite to see what other things ought to be considered as part of your precatechumenate catechesis.

The Rite of Acceptance Into the Order of Catechumens

The Rite of Acceptance Into the Order of Catechumens is the first major rite of the Rite of Christian Initiation of Adults. It is the culmination of the period of evangelization and precatechumenate, and it is the doorway through which inquirers enter the catechumenate.

The Rite of Acceptance is a celebration of the initial conversion of the candidates, and it is the Church's way of accepting the children "who intend to become its members" (#41). Moreover, the rite is the first time the candidates assemble publicly before the parish community. The community affirms its desire for them to continue their journey of conversion. The Church also pledges support to the candidates (#53).

An adaptation for children of the Rite of Acceptance Into the Order of Catechumens is found in the first section of Part II (#260-276) of the Rite of Christian Initiation of Adults. The structure of the rite for children is very similar to the adult rite found in Part I (#48-68). There are, however, some notable exceptions.

First, in the adaptation for children, the First Acceptance of the Gospel, which is found in the adult rite immediately after the Opening Dialogue, is omitted. Instead, there is a "brief catechesis" as part of the opening dialogue. This brief catechesis describes for the children "the step they are taking." Unlike the adult rite, the children are not asked to make a verbal response when accepting the gospel. Apparently, the authors of the rite felt that children could not understand such a heavy responsibility as accepting the gospel.

Since the children are being asked to walk with Christ, however, and are mature enough to prepare for baptism, they ought to be afforded the opportunity to accept the gospel for themselves. It is my belief that the omission of the First Acceptance of the Gospel is one of many examples of the children's rite being unnecessarily watered down. The authors of the rite, with the best of intentions, I'm sure, probably did not want to ask too much of the children.

Having the children personally accept the Gospel would be more consistent with the adult rite in Part I. A simple adaptation would be to include a suitable First Acceptance of the Gospel (#52) after the Opening Dialogue and to omit the brief catechesis found at the end of #264.

A second difference between the structure of the adult rite and the adaptation for children is that the adult rite sees the possibility of the rite being celebrated at the community's Eucharist, from which the catechumens would be dismissed (#68). However, the children's adaptation does not seem to see this as normative because #261 says that the children's "celebration is not normally combined with the celebration of the Eucharist." If the rite for children is not normally combined with the celebration of the

Eucharist, then the Sunday assembly does not celebrate with the children. This raises pressing questions about where and when and how to celebrate the rite with children.

The Rite Within the Celebration of Sunday Eucharist

One reason the Rite recommends that the celebration not normally be combined with the celebration of the Eucharist is that a celebration of the Eucharist would likely include the Sunday assembly, where a relatively large number of people would be present. The Rite repeatedly recommends that the liturgical rites for children "be celebrated with an actively participating but small congregation, since the presence of a large group might make the children uncomfortable" (#260, also see #257).[9]

In my experience, I have found that children are very comfortable when they celebrate the rite with large numbers of people at Sunday worship. In general, children like being the center of attention. They like being the "special ones" in the procession and in the front seats. And the presence of parents and sponsors adds a sense of security that helps them feel even more comfortable.

Another good reason to celebrate the rite during Sunday Eucharist is the witness the children and the assembly provide to one another. First, the presence of children and their families is a testimony to the community. The assembly sees that children and adults alike have made a commitment to walk the journey of conversion with Jesus Christ. They see youngsters asking to become members of the community, and they are led to wonder, "What is it about this Church that makes a twelve-year-old want to join?" and "Why do I stay?"

The assembly gives witness to the children

as well. The Sunday assembly gathered in worship is a primary manifestation of the Body of Christ. Child catechumens learn something of the Body of Christ when they are in the midst of the Sunday assembly. The young catechumens need to experience the Body of Christ as it is manifested in their own community. Although the Body of Christ is certainly made manifest in other places and other ways, the Sunday Eucharist is the Body of Christ par excellence. To keep the children separate in a small celebration denies both them and the larger community an opportunity of forming one another in faith.

Celebrating the Rite With Adult Catechumens

An issue related to celebrating the rite with a small or large group is the question of whether children should celebrate with adult catechumens. The presence of a separate rite in Part II implies that a separate rite for children is preferred. However, separating child catechumens from adult catechumens gives the impression that there are two separate processes of initiation: one for children and one for adults. But only one process of initiation exists for adults and children of catechetical age. Celebrating the rite together reinforces that fact.

In addition, there are times when the children's parents are also candidates for initiation. Since the journey of conversion should be a family-based process and the celebration of the rite is a major step on the journey, the family needs to remain together for the celebration of the rite. To separate the family at two different rites would be divisive.

In general, children and adults celebrate together and the adult rite (#48-68) is used. Some adaptation needs to be made in order to

accommodate the children, their parents and sponsors. For example, during the Affirmation by the Sponsors and the Assembly, the children's adaptation asks the parents to give their consent to the children's request for Baptism (#265). The questions directed to the parents can easily be added to the adult rite. Also, some of the language in the children's adaptation has been simplified. Although the language in the adult rite is not especially difficult, the presiding minister will want to be conscious of developmentally appropriate language for children and make adaptations where necessary.

Celebrating With Child Catechumens and Candidates

Another question to be addressed is whether children who are baptized candidates for full communion with the Roman Catholic Church should celebrate with child catechumens. As with adults, children who are baptized candidates for full communion with the Catholic Church may also celebrate an adapted version of this rite. Although there are no specific combined rites for children, the combined rites found in Appendix I of the *Rite* may be adapted and used with children.

The Celebration of the Rite With Children

Receiving the Children

When the rite begins, the children are to be waiting with their parents and/or sponsors "at the entrance of the place chosen for the celebration" (#261). "The celebration takes place in the church or in a place that, according to the age and understanding of the children, can help them to experience a warm welcome" (#261). If the celebration takes place outside of the Sunday Eucharist, then the place for the celebration might be a chapel or a space in the catechetical center or Catholic school that is conducive to worship.

Paragraph 262 refers to the children "waiting with their parents or guardians or, alternatively, with their sponsors." In this case, the sponsors are seen as those "who act on this occasion for the parent and present the children" when the parents are not present (#260). In other words, the parents present their children, like an adult sponsor would present an adult. However, if there are parish sponsors or sponsoring families who are active in the process in addition to the parents, then they would also participate in the rite.

Greeting

The celebrant greets the children, their families and sponsors. Although the rite does not call for a specific introduction at this point, parents should introduce their children to the community. Or, sponsors could also introduce the family, especially if the parents are candidates themselves.

Opening Dialogue

After the greeting, the children express their intentions in the opening dialogue. The rite (#264) calls for the children to state their intention in their own words or through a question-and-answer format. I strongly recommend that the children use their own words to express themselves. Personal expression of one's intention is a much more powerful witness than rote repetition of a standard response. Many children feel quite strongly about their desire to become members of the Church. Others feel they want to know more about God or Jesus Christ. Some children simply say they want to be baptized.

Nonetheless, reflection and preparation prior to the rite is necessary. With adequate preparation, even young children can articulate their intentions. However, if a child is overly apprehensive about speaking to a group, a parent or sponsor should speak for the child.

(Candidates' First Acceptance of the Gospel)

Although the children's adaptation of the Rite of Acceptance Into the Order of Catechumens does not call for the child to publicly accept the gospel, it can be easily included at this point. And, if children and adults are celebrating together, it is already included in the rite. The First Acceptance of the Gospel (#52) can be adapted from the given text, or better yet, the thoughts and ideas from the children's opening dialogue can be used.

For example, in the opening dialogue, one of the candidates might have said, "People here have been really nice to me, and I want to be baptized so I can be a member of this church." Then, during the First Acceptance of the Gospel, the celebrant repeats what the candidates have said. The celebrant might say, "Candidates, you have testified that the people of this community have been very nice, open and friendly toward you. You expressed a desire to be one of us. Are you ready to live the life of a Christian?" If there are a large number of candidates, including the responses of all may be difficult. In those instances, an adaptation of the text given in #52 may be more appropriate.

Affirmation by the Parents (Sponsors) and the Assembly

At this point, the parents are asked to give their consent for their children's request for Baptism. Also, if baptized children are preparing for Confirmation and Eucharist, their parents would also give consent for their preparation. In #265, the children are asked to bring their parents forward to give their assent. In all likelihood, however, their parents have been standing with them since the introductions and opening dialogue.

If the rite is combined with the celebration for adults, the questions addressed to parents (#265) easily fit with the questions addressed to the adults' sponsors (#53). Thus, the children's parents, the sponsors and the assembly are asked to give their support to the children.

Signing of the Candidates With the Cross

Although the rite calls for the signing of the forehead and other senses prior to the Liturgy of the Word (#266-268), many liturgists and those with pastoral experience implementing the rite, find the signing is more appropriately placed after the homily. In this way, the candidates are in the main body of the church and can more easily be seen by the assembly. Secondly, they have heard the Gospel message and then accept the cross of Christ, rather than accepting the cross before they hear the Gospel.

Wherever the signing is placed, it is an important and meaningful gesture for the children. The parents who sign their children also find it to be a significant moment. One father spoke of how he felt "humbled" as he knelt to sign the feet of his son. Sponsors and siblings may also sign the candidates with the sign of the cross.

Though the "Signing of the Other Senses" is bracketed to indicate that it is optional, I strongly recommend it be included in any celebration with children. The prayers for the signing of the other senses (#268) are simpler and somewhat milder in the children's adaptation than they are in the adult rite (#56). Here again is an example of children getting a weaker version of the adult rite. Nonetheless, when adults and children celebrate together, the prayers in #56 are appropriate for all.

Invitation to the Celebration of the Word of God

The presider invites the children and their parents and sponsors to enter the church or the place chosen for the celebration. Paragraph 269 calls for the children to take their place "with their parents or sponsors or with the baptized companions of their catechetical group" (see #254.1). Generally, the candidates would already be with their parents or sponsors. Their "baptized companions," however, may be present for the celebration, and, as such, the candidates and families might also sit with the baptized companions.

Instruction, Readings, Homily, Presentation of a Bible

The Liturgy of the Word follows as given in the ritual text (#270-276). After the homily, there is the option of presenting "a book containing the gospels" to the children" (#273). This book could be a Bible, a children's Bible, a book of the Gospels, a book containing the lectionary readings or the children's lectionary readings. I recommend that a Bible or a book of lectionary readings be given, rather than a children's Bible because the children should become accustomed to hearing, reading and using the word of God as it is proclaimed in the liturgy. When a Bible or book of lectionary readings is presented, we promote a consistency among the liturgy, what is read at home and what is used for breaking open the word. I also give each family a copy of *At Home with the Word* (Liturgy Training Publications) or another publication that contains the weekly lectionary readings. This helps each family prepare for the weekly session and allows them to refer to the readings later.

Intercessions for the Children

The intercessions given in #274 can be adapted to fit the needs of the children and the community.

Prayer Over the Children, Dismissal

The rite concludes with the children being dismissed. If the Eucharist is being celebrated, the children are dismissed to break open the word and subsequently to break open the rite with their families and sponsors. Otherwise, a song concludes the rite and the children are dismissed to reflect upon the word and the rite.

Catechetical Implications of the Rite

Certain key elements of the rite have catechetical implications: the children's acceptance by the community, the presentation of and signing with the cross and the proclamation of the word of God. The importance of these elements in the rite means that they most definitely were given attention during the preceding period of the precatechumenate. For example, the children would have shown an interest in the community before asking to be considered among its potential members. They would have given some thought to the meaning of the cross before their bodies are covered by it. And, they would have some familiarity with God's word before accepting it from the community.

Moreover, the Opening Dialogue (#264) also has implications for catechesis because the children are asked, "What do you want to become?" The given response is, "a Christian." This short exchange says a great deal about what is presumed to have happened before the children reached the celebration of the rite. The children must have learned something of who a Christian is if they are able to say they want to be one. The children must have heard stories about Christians of the present and of the past. They must have heard stories about Christians and their ancestors from the Christian and Hebrew Scriptures. They must have seen Christians from their parish and

from other parishes living as followers of Jesus.

Similarly, the children are asked, "Why do you want to become a Christian?" They reply, "Because I believe in Christ." If the children are saying that they believe in Christ, then they must have learned something of who Christ is. They must have heard stories from the Scriptures and stories from present day Christianity about who Christ is. These stories make up the "catechetical content" of the period of evangelization and precatechumenate.

The Rite of Acceptance Into the Order of Catechumens, then, implies that acceptance by the community, the cross, the word of God, being a Christian and knowing Jesus Christ have been part of the catechesis of the period of evangelization and precatechumenate. As each initiation team prays, studies and reflects upon the Rite of Acceptance Into the Order of Catechumens, other indicators for catechesis will emerge.

Preparing Children for the Rite of Acceptance Into the Order of Catechumens

Discerning readiness: When to celebrate the Rite with children. Gone are the days when every parish celebrated the Rite of Acceptance into the Order of Catechumens on the first Sunday of Advent. (At least I hope that's true!) A close reading of the Rite shows that the proper time to celebrate the Rite of Acceptance with children and adults is when "the beginnings of the spiritual life and the fundamentals of Christian teaching have taken root in the candidates" (#42). In other words, the rite is celebrated when the children are "ready," rather than at a predetermined time.

Since the section of the rite that deals with

children does not specifically address the readiness of children to celebrate the rite, you must return to Part I for guidance. In Part I (#42), you will find in addition to "the beginnings of the spiritual life and the fundamentals of Christian teaching" having taken root in the candidates, there must also be:

- evidence of first faith;
- initial conversion;
- intention to change;
- intention to enter into a relationship with God in Christ;
- the first stirrings of repentance;
- a start to the practice of calling upon God in prayer;
- a sense of the Church;
- some experience of the company and spirit of Christians through contact with a priest or with members of the community.

At first glance, all these criteria may seem like a great deal to expect of a child. However, all these criteria are to be considered in a way that is developmentally appropriate for the child's age and maturity. "The first stirrings of repentance" in a eight-year-old child will look different, for instance, than that in a thirty-eight-year-old adult. Nonetheless, we still have the responsibility of setting aside "sufficient and necessary time" to "evaluate, and, if necessary, to purify the candidates' motives and dispositions" before the celebration of the rite (#43).

When determining a child's readiness for the rite, you should note that the criteria given in #42 indicate that the beginnings of true conversion are showing forth in the child. Please notice that the description of readiness includes the words *evidence, initial, intention, first stirrings, a start, a sense.* In other words, a dramatic change in a child is not necessary in order for that child to celebrate the Rite of Acceptance Into the Order of Catechumens.

The Church looks for a few indicators that point to a child's "initial conversion."

One way for initiation team members to discern readiness for the rite is simply to talk with the child, parent and sponsor about the child's readiness. If you are leading this "discernment interview," talk with the child, parent and sponsor about how the initiation journey has had an effect on the child's life. Try to discover in what ways the child deepened her or his relationship with God in Jesus Christ. Does the child have a desire to become part of the Church? Are there signs of initial conversion, e.g., changes in attitude, understanding or behavior?

You should discuss these questions in a comfortable, informal setting. The discussion should be more of a conversation than an interview. Also, informal observations made by team members, sponsors and parents contribute to the discernment process.

The Rite of Acceptance itself also gives indications about what is expected of the children prior to celebration of the rite. Examine the questions that are asked of the children and their expected answers.

The criteria given in #42 and in the rite itself give the initiation team guidelines when determining a child's readiness for the celebration of the Rite of Acceptance into the Order of Catechumens. For a sample "discernment interview" guide, see the appendix, pages 134-136.

Sample Session

A Preparation Session for the Rite of Acceptance Into the Order of Catechumens

The remote preparation for the rite is the entire period of evangelization and precatechumenate, since everything that happens in the first period culminates in the Rite of Acceptance Into the Order of Catechumens. The discernment process or interview is also part of the preparation for the rite, since it helps the child and family reflect on their readiness. The purpose of the proximate preparation for the rite is to help the children and their families celebrate well.

The preparation session is also part of the larger process of liturgical catechesis. The session is meant to prepare and lead participants to a full and proper participation in the liturgy. As such, the preparation session focuses around the symbols of the rite and the lectionary readings that will be proclaimed during the rite. The session should also be designed to meet the needs of the particular group of catechumens who will be celebrating the rite. Even though not every symbol and every reading needs direct attention during the preparation session, the cross, the word and the acceptance of the candidates are primary elements of the rite. Here is a sample preparation session in which the cross is a primary element:

- Gathering and Introduction
- God's Story and My Story
- Reflection on the Cross
- Connecting With the Rite
- Closing Ritual

Gathering and Introduction

Warmly greet each child by name. Begin by reminding the children and families about what has been said in previous weeks and months about being a follower of Jesus. The children should be helped to remember what they, their companions, sponsors or parents have said about being a follower of Jesus. Recall with the children Scripture readings that were discussed in previous sessions regarding Jesus' followers.

God's Story and My Story

Read or tell the story of John 1:35-42. (This Gospel is used in the celebration of the rite if it is celebrated outside a Sunday Eucharist. Or, use another reading that will be heard during the rite.) John the Baptizer sees Jesus and exclaims, "Behold, the Lamb of God!" Jesus says to two of the disciples, "Come and see."

In small groups, made up of the family and the sponsoring family, invite the children and adults to read the story again (provide copies). Then, discuss the following questions:

- If you were one of the disciples present that day and Jesus asked you, "What do you seek?" how would you answer? What do you want to ask from Jesus?
- What does being a follower of Jesus mean to you?

After discussing in small groups, ask the small groups to share with the large group.

Reflection on the Cross

Prior to the beginning of the session, you have enthroned the cross in the center of the room or in a prominent place. The Bible or lectionary is also present. Talk with the children and adults about the cross being part of the life of a disciple. Following Jesus means following him all the way on his journey, a journey that included his death on the cross. All of our lives have crosses. Everyone has a difficulty, hurt or pain that they bear. Some crosses are bigger than others.

Invite the children, their families and sponsoring families to discuss the following questions in small groups:

■ How is the cross present in your life?
■ How is the cross present in your family?
■ How will Jesus help you?

A generous amount of time is needed to discuss these poignant questions about the cross. Children, like adults, may need some time to sit and think before they want to share a burden or pain they are experiencing.

Mindy, an eleven-year-old Mexican-American, who had recently moved to the Midwest with her family, said that the cross she bore was being made fun of for the color of her skin. She told a group of other young candidates that when she first moved to her present school, girls wrote her notes saying, "Nobody likes you. Why don't you go back to where you came from?" Even though Mindy had made some friends in her new school, the pain inflicted by the other girls was a big cross in her life.

For the discussion, the small groups might be made up of candidate families and sponsoring families. Or, the children might be in small groups and the adults in separate small groups. Some children feel freer to discuss crosses in their family if they are not with their parents. After the small-group sharing, each group is invited to share with the larger group. Participants share only as they are comfortable.

After all have shared, you should speak to the children and their families about the fact that accepting our crosses is part of discipleship. The good news of the cross is that even though the cross may be painful, God promises that a cross leads to new life. Just as Jesus rose to new life from death on a cross, our crosses will ultimately lead to new life, too.

Connecting With the Rite

Tell the children that the parish will be celebrating their acceptance into the community. Being accepted into the Church means accepting the way of Jesus. Explain that their acceptance into the Church makes them a catechumen, that is, a person who is preparing to become a Christian. Explain the difference between a catechumen and candidate. Ask the children to give some serious thought to why they want to be a Christian. Describe how, during the rite, they will be asked to tell the parish why they want to become a Christian.

Then, give the children questions that will help them think about why they want to become a members of the community. Their responses to these questions will be part of the Opening Dialogue during the celebration of the rite:

■ Why do you want to become a Christian? Or, why do you want to follow Jesus?
■ What do you want the Christian community, the Church, to do for you?

(The questions are adaptations of the questions that will be asked of the children during the rite [#264].)

Depending on whether the preparation session is a "retreat day" or a two-hour session, the children may want to take the questions home and discuss them with their parents. If the preparation session is an extended day for a family retreat, then the children and their families and sponsoring families are given a generous amount of time to take a walk and reflect on the questions. When they return, ask them to share their responses to the questions with you and the whole group.

Closing Ritual

The session concludes with a closing prayer and a song that will be used in the celebration of the rite. Or, there could be a celebration of the word with one of the readings from the rite being used.

Invite the group to stand.

Catechist (with hands outstretched): Let us pray.

> Gracious God,
> you have called these children, and they
>   have answered.
> Look with favor upon them as they journey
>   ever closer to you.
> May their families and this community
>   support them on their way.
> We ask this through Christ our Lord.
> Amen.

Close with an appropriate song.

Rehearsing for the Rite of Acceptance Into the Order of Catechumens

At some point, the liturgist (or, if there is not a parish liturgist, whoever is responsible for the celebration of the rite) "walks through" the rite with the parents and the sponsors. Care needs to be taken when reviewing the signing of the senses with the parents. Parents need to know how to use their hands properly when making the sign of the cross on the child's senses. Also, each family and sponsor should be standing in such a way so that they can be seen by the community. If children are in the front of church with their backs to the assembly, no one can see them. However, if the children are positioned throughout the church, then members of the assembly can see the child's wonder and parents' deep devotion as the child is covered with the cross.

Also at the rehearsal, the liturgist or catechist can assist the parents in how best to prepare their child to speak during the

Opening Dialogue. The parents can reassure the child that a simple response can be given as to why they want to become a Christian and what they ask of the Church. If a child is especially apprehensive about speaking publicly, then the parent may speak for the child, or the child may wish to read from a note card.

Do not rehearse with the children. As long as their parents and sponsors are comfortable with the rite, the children will feel comfortable also. Moreover, the children will feel more comfortable and will respond with greater ease if they have a prior relationship with the presider. Ideally, the presiding celebrant has participated in some of the sessions and has spent some time getting to know the candidates and their families. Knowing each child by name is an obvious advantage.

Reflection Session After the Rite of Acceptance Into the Order of Catechumens

In liturgical catechesis, the "unpacking" or "breaking open" of the liturgical rite after its celebration is the step that completes the process. Most often, when the rite is done well, its celebration is an intense, formative, faith-enriching experience for children. They are eager to talk about how they felt, what they saw, what they heard, what was said, what it meant. After the celebration of the rite, the children gather with the catechist to talk about their experience of the rite. Their families, companions and sponsors will join them after Mass has ended.

The purpose of breaking open, or unpacking, the rite is to help the new catechumens and candidates name what they experienced in the rite and then name what that experience means. By naming their experience, the children come to a better understanding of their initiation journey and how God is calling them. The most effective way to help the children articulate their feelings and the meaning of the rite is to focus on the major symbols of the rite. Symbols speak to us in ways that words alone cannot.

Two questions will help the children unpack the experience:

■ How did you feel?
■ What did it mean?

If you focus on these questions and let the children speak freely (staying out of the Holy Spirit's way), the children will come to a clearer realization of what it means to be accepted as a catechumen or candidate. Keeping the children attuned to these questions will help focus the discussion on the meaning of the rite. Although you should first invite the children to talk about how they felt during the rite, the movement of the two questions flows back and forth. The discussion is circular rather than linear as the children may talk about meaning as they share their feelings.

When Mass has ended, parents, sponsors and companions join the children for further reflection on the rite. Immediately after Mass, however, time should be allowed for parishioners to greet the children and their families. This is usually done at a juice, coffee and doughnut reception.

After an ample time for refreshments and socializing, the catechumens, candidates, families, sponsors and companions gather to break open the rite. The space for the gathering could be the same place where the children break open the word, or if another place is needed, the environment should be such that it connects to the rite. For example, you could enthrone the lectionary, light a candle and have a cross prominent in the room. Here is a sample session:

Sample Session

■ Gathering
■ How Did You Feel?
■ What Did It Mean?
■ Summation and Closure

Gathering

As the children and their families enter, encourage them to sit with their families and their sponsoring families.

How Did You Feel?

Begin by inviting all those present to relax and remember the rite they just celebrated. A meditation style reflection recalls the celebration. Music from the ritual may be used.

Catechist: Remember now how you felt as:

■ you waited outside church with your mom, dad, sponsors (you waited with your child by your side);
■ your mom or dad or sponsor introduced you (you introduced the candidate);
■ you told the parish why you wanted to be a Christian;
■ your mom, dad and/or sponsor signed your eyes, ears, feet with the sign of the cross (you signed the senses of your child);
■ you were given the Bible;
■ you processed out of church.

Next, invite the children to share one or two words that describe how they felt during the rite. After the children have had the opportunity to speak, invite the parents and sponsors to share their feelings about the rite. Encourage everyone to share only their feelings at this point.

I have found that children respond in both predictable and surprising ways to the question, "How did you feel?" Some of the more predictable responses are:

- I felt happy.
- I felt special.
- I was nervous.
- I felt people were glad to see us.

Some of the more surprising responses I have heard are:

- I felt holy.
- I felt really strong.
- I felt a lot of support.
- I felt big. When my parents bent down to sign my feet, it was like they were saying they would be loyal to me. I just felt like I was the big person.
- I felt like Jesus was covering me. Like he was saying he would always be with me.

Sometimes, the responses don't come easily. You may need to ask the children more specific questions, for example, "How did you feel when we were standing outside waiting to come in the church?" Or "How did you feel as your mom or dad signed your eyes? Your ears?" This helps the children focus on a specific part of the rite.

In addition to encouraging the children to share how they felt during the rite, you should also invite the parents and sponsors to share their responses to the rite. There is power in these rites for everyone involved. Often a parent's or sponsor's experience is as deeply felt as that of the children. Also, their testimony shared during the reflection session is a further witness to the children that God is at work in the liturgy and in the lives of their families. The parent and sponsor frequently speak not only about their personal feelings but also about the feelings of commitment, pride, devotion and loyalty they have toward their child. This is affirming testimony for the children.

What Did It Mean?

The feelings that the children and families name lead into a discussion about what the rite meant. To get behind the feelings and unpack what the rite meant to the children and to their families, I usually ask a follow-up question after they describe how they felt. For example, when Andy said that he felt strong, I later came back to him and asked him, "What made you feel strong, Andy?" After giving the question some thought, Andy replied, "Having all those people around us, smiling and looking at us. It just made me feel really strong." Indeed, feeling strengthened and accepted by the community are important aspects of the rite. The "symbol" of the community had spoken clearly to Andy.

You don't necessarily need to ask directly, "What does it mean?" In using his own words, Andy articulated an important aspect of the rite. He had grasped the importance of being accepted by the community.

At other times, however, you will need to be specific in your questions to the children. When children speak in general terms about feeling "good" or "happy," then you will want to ask a more specific question like, "What does it mean to you that your mom signed you all over with the sign of the cross?" Or, "What does it say to you that everyone clapped after your grandfather introduced you?"

Sometimes the children freely add their description of meaning along with their feeling words or phrases. For instance, when Mike described feeling "big," he quickly added that the signing of his feet by his parents was the reason he felt this way. To him this meant that his parents would be loyal. In other words, his parents would support him in his Christian way of life. Mike, too, had grasped a meaning of the rite.

There are also times when the children may say little after the celebration of a rite. Whatever the reason for not sharing, you must respect the child's choice not to share. Some candidates need more distance and time away from the rite before they are ready to share. When children are silent, there is no reason for you to be uncomfortable. Most children are quite comfortable with silence, and the silence gives them a chance for further reflection. You do not need to fill the silence with explanatory comments about the rite. Instead, if the children choose to be silent after you have asked the appropriate questions, then you should allow the silence to stand for some time before moving the reflection to another part of the rite.

At times, however, a lack of sharing after a rite may happen if the rite was improperly or poorly celebrated, if the symbols of rite were weak, if the presider was ill-prepared and impersonal, if the inquirers had not adequately discerned the initial conversion called for to become catechumens. If this is the case, then the intiation team will need to gather to evaluate the rite and make changes for the future.

Summation and Closure

After the children and adults have had ample opportunity to reflect on the meaning of the rite, you should summarize what has been said. Return to the experience and the comments of the group and highlight the important elements of the rite. Don't make this movement academic; just sum up what the children and their families experienced. Here are some of the highlights that you should look for in the remarks of the children and families:

- acceptance by the community;
- the community's pledge to support the catechumens and candidates;
- acceptance of the cross;
- acceptance of the gospel;
- desire to learn more about Jesus and the Church.

You may also need to address questions that arise out of the celebration of the rite. Depending upon the nature of the question, it might best be dealt with at a subsequent session. For example, if questions arise about the meaning of the Jesus' cross, you should tell the group that you'll discuss those questions the following week. End this session with a song from the rite itself.

Pointing Ahead

The children have now passed through the first doorway (#6) and entered the period of the catechumenate. Just as the Rite of Acceptance Into the Order of Catechumens is a culmination of the preceding period, it also points ahead to the period of the catechumenate. Some of the ritual high points—acceptance, cross and word—imply that the same will be considered more seriously during the period of the catechumenate. Indeed, through a process of "suitable pastoral formation" the children will learn the Christian way of life.

Summary

The period of evangelization and precatechumenate is a time for evangelizing young inquirers and their families. During this period, the most important way evangelization happens is through storytelling. Proclaiming the Good News by sharing the stories of our Christian tradition awakens in young inquirers their natural affinity for the holy. Lastly, the Rite of Acceptance Into the Order of Catechumens is a high point in the children's journey of conversion. Not only is the rite a culmination of the period of evangelization and precatechumenate, but it is also the doorway through which the children step into the second period, the period of the catechumenate.

REFERENCES

[1] Pope Paul VI, Apostolic Exhortation, "On Evangelization in the Modern World": *Evangelii Nuntiandi*, 8 December 1975, #17.

[2] Ibid., #18.

[3] Avery Dulles, "John Paul II and the New Evangelization," *America*, 1 February 1992, pp. 57-58.

[4] Robert Coles, *The Spiritual Life of Children* (Boston: Houghton Mifflin Company, 1990), pp. 36-37.

[5] Ibid., p. 128.

[6] Ibid., p. 36.

[7] Raymond E. Brown, S.S., Joseph A. Fitzmeyer, S.J., Roland E. Murphy, O. Carm., eds. *The New Jerome Biblical Commentary* (Englewood Cliffs, N.J.: Prentice Hall, 1990), p. 20.

[8] "On Evangelization in the Modern World," #17.

[9] Many liturgists speculate that the reason for this odd recommendation of keeping children away from large assemblies has to do with the authorship of the Rite. The German mentality of the authors is reflected in this type of thinking about children. In the German culture children might be more apt to be overwhelmed by a large crowd.

 *Notes*

4

The Period of the Catechumenate

On the Seventh Sunday in Ordinary Time, during the period of the catechumenate, the child catechumens, candidates, families, companions and sponsoring families at Our Lady of Good Counsel Parish were talking about a time when someone in their families needed or asked for forgiveness. The family session followed the children's breaking open the word, which had centered around Mark 2:1-12, the story of Jesus forgiving and healing the paralyzed man.

As the discussion progressed, obvious friction was erupting in the Austin family. I sat down with the group and asked how everyone was doing. Lisa, the mother, started to describe how she wished her children would just admit when they are wrong and ask for forgiveness. Brad snapped right back at his mom with a remark about her not hearing what he was trying to say. The discussion quickly escalated into a family argument. After a few awkward moments, the family temporarily resolved the issue at hand. The ongoing need for and importance of reconciliation had been made evident in our midst.

The story illustrates several important aspects of the period of the catechumenate with children. First, the catechumenal process is family-centered, as it was during the period of evangelization and precatechumenate. Second, catechumenate catechesis flows from the Sunday readings. The Liturgy of the Word is followed by a session in which children break open the word and then, after Mass, there is an extended catechesis with the families. Third, the story illustrates how a discussion that has the word of God as its point of departure can touch the real-life issues of children and families. The catechumenate can and does bring up some hard issues for families. The "real life" discussions that start with the word are at the center of catechumenate catechesis. Fourth, the story shows that the catechumenate process is always surprising and cannot be completely planned or programmed.

Suitable Pastoral Formation for Children

What the story does not illustrate is the breadth and depth of the formation process during the period of the catechumenate. The story depicts one family-centered catechumenate session. It shows one part of the four-part formation process for child catechumens and candidates. Here are the four elements that make up the entire process of "suitable pastoral formation" as called for in the Rite (#75).

The Rite does not give any directives or guidelines specifically for children during the catechumenate. It intends for Part I to be the guide (see National Statute 18).

The Rite describes the period of the catechumenate as "an extended period during which the candidates are given suitable pastoral formation and guidance, aimed at training them in the Christian way of life" (#75). There are several key phrases here. First, the catechumenate is "an extended period." This echoes #253, which says that children's initiation is to be "extended over several years, if need be." The Rite is emphasizing that the initiation of adults and children is a gradual process and not meant to be rushed through in a few months. Further, National Statute 6 says that the period of the catechumenate should last at least one year.

During this extended period of time, the child catechumens are to receive a "suitable pastoral formation."[1] Catechumens, then, are to be given much more than catechetical formation, though catechesis is part of their formation, which is to be "suited" to their age. They are to be formed in faith through catechesis, the community, liturgical rites and apostolic works.

Suitable Catechesis

The Rite describes the "four ways" in which the catechumens are given "suitable pastoral formation." The first is a "suitable catechesis" that is "gradual and complete in its coverage, accommodated to the liturgical year, and solidly supported by celebrations of the word" (#75.1). The catechesis is to give an "appropriate acquaintance with dogmas and precepts," but it also leads to a "profound sense of the mystery of salvation." In being accommodated to the liturgical year and supported by celebrations of the word, the Rite seems to indicate that the catechesis it envisions should make use of the lectionary.

By using the lectionary, catechesis is "gradual and complete." Moreover, catechesis

does not become a class on Catholic doctrine. The catechetical model that I prefer uses the Sunday lectionary readings as its starting point. "Breaking open the word" is extended to include a fuller catechesis based on the readings. This catechetical method is sometimes called "lectionary-based catechesis."

The Christian Community

The second way that the faith of the children is brought to maturity is through the help and example of the Christian community (#75.2). By its example, the entire community helps the children learn the Christian way of life. First and foremost, the worshiping assembly gathered for Eucharist on Sunday is the best example of "Christian community" the candidates will ever see. The Sunday assembly is the Body of Christ at its best. Thus, candidates need to experience this manifestation of Christ's Body by participating in the Liturgy of the Word. The assembly gathered for other types of public worship also gives witness to the candidates.

Specifically, the Rite says that the catechumens are to learn from the community about prayer, about how to witness to their faith and about how to "practice love of neighbor." Children will learn these Christian practices by spending time with their sponsors and companions at parish events as well as outside the parish proper. By participating in parish activities, the child catechumens and their families see how Christians live and work with one another. The sponsoring family may invite the catechumenal family to join them in attending the parish festival or the pancake breakfast. Going with parish friends helps the catechumenal family to feel more comfortable. Also, by participating in parish events, the child catechumens can meet and interact with their peers. Older children who are companions or sponsors might invite catechumens to teen social events, service projects or discussion nights.

Informal time spent with sponsors or sponsoring families outside the parish proper is also helpful for the catechumens and candidates. Sponsoring families might invite their catechumenal family over for lunch one Sunday or for dinner one evening. One family pair (the catechumenal family and the sponsoring family) that I worked with began a tradition of going out for brunch at the local Big Boy Restaurant after the Sunday sessions.

Sponsors might also invite the catechumenal family to some other outside activity like the local high school basketball game. The ages and interests of the children will determine the activities that the families have in common. Spending time together allows the children and parents to see how Catholic Christian families function. Mostly, the catechumens will see a family just like their own. On the other hand, it is hoped that the catechumens will see something that makes the Christian family a little different. Treating family members with respect and dignity, treating others fairly, working for justice and peace, showing kindness and being helpful, prayerful and courteous are just a few of the attitudes and behaviors that catechumens and parents can learn from their sponsors.

Sponsors may also want to invite and encourage the candidates and their families to pray and worship with the community at times other than Sunday Eucharist. Familiarizing the candidates with various types of prayer and worship is a good responsibility for the sponsor to assume. For example, inviting the candidates and their families to Morning Prayer or Evening Prayer introduces this ancient liturgical prayer of the Church to the families. Similarly, inviting the catechumen's family to a Marian prayer time in May or Stations of the Cross during Lent introduces Catholic devotional practices to the catechumenal family.

Also, sponsors and sponsoring families can model personal and family prayer for the catechumens and their families. Seeing a sponsoring family pray grace before a meal or praying together around the Advent wreath helps the catechumens and their parents "learn to turn more readily to God in prayer" (#75.2). A sponsor or sponsoring family might also teach a catechumenal family about the rosary or other favorite devotions or prayers. The sponsor or the catechist may also suggest that the child catechumen keep a journal of her or his initiation journey. The sponsoring family shares whatever comes naturally to them. Yet, in some situations, the sponsor coordinator may need to encourage sponsors to pray with their catechumens or candidates or give them ideas on what and how to share their prayer life.

Suitable Liturgical Rites

The third way the Church forms its young catechumens is "by means of suitable liturgical rites" (#75.3). The child catechumens participate in the major rites of acceptance and election, in the minor rites of the period of the catechumenate, and in the rites belonging to the period of purification and enlightenment. Although the first section of Part II of the Rite does not have all these rites adapted for children, the rites in Part I may be adapted for children. Celebrating the rites helps to "purify" and "strengthen" the young catechumens (#75.3). Liturgy plays a central role in the life of Catholics and thus must be central when the Church is forming young catechumens and candidates.[2]

The Rite particularly mentions celebrations

of the word that "are arranged" for the catechumens (#75.3). These celebrations, described more fully in #81-89, are specifically for the catechumens. Celebrations of the word may be on a weekday or at whatever time is convenient for child catechumens and their families. They may also be held in conjunction with catechetical instruction (#81). There may also be special celebrations of the word in the Catholic school.

Also, the Sunday Liturgy of the Word is one of the celebrations for the catechumens. The Rite calls for the catechumens to be "kindly dismissed before the liturgy of the Eucharist begins" (#75.3). Children are dismissed with adults but usually meet separately to break open the word. Even this act of dismissal is formative in its nature. By dismissing the children before the Liturgy of the Eucharist, the Church is saying to those in formation that preparation for reception of the Eucharist is extremely important. Reflecting on God's word and experiencing Christ present in the word is a serious form of preparation for the Eucharist. Likewise, hospitality dictates that one does not invite guests to a meal only to refuse to let them partake. Thus, dismissing children to reflect upon the word is proper preparation for their eventual reception of Eucharist.

A special case regarding child catechumens and their dismissal before the Liturgy of the Eucharist occurs in the Catholic school setting. Most Catholic schools celebrate the Eucharist with their students and typically all students attend Mass at some point. Especially in elementary schools, an "all school Mass" or a "grade-level Mass" is common. When child catechumens and candidates are present at these Masses, they should be dismissed prior to the Liturgy of Eucharist, just as they are on Sunday. Likewise, they should meet with a catechist for breaking open the word just as they do following a Sunday dismissal.

Apostolic Works

The fourth way the Church forms its catechumens, including its young ones, is through apostolic work with others (#75.4). In other words, the children learn the life of Christian service by working along with Christians. This is not to say that "service hours" are assigned to children as part of their catechumenal formation. Rather, by working with parishioners to write letters to legislators, or by visiting people who are "shut-ins," or by grooming the parish grounds or stocking the food pantry, children learn that a life of serving others is part of living the gospel.

In addition to working with parishioners in the parish setting, sponsors or sponsoring families may invite the catechumens and their families to join them in some work outside of the parish. At St. Margaret Parish, one sponsoring family invited the catechumen they were sponsoring to go with them and others from the parish to the neighborhood shelter to serve lunch one Saturday morning a month. This afforded the opportunity for the young catechumen to work with one of her peers (the daughter in the sponsoring family) and with other Christians. It also provided a chance for the sponsoring family to spend time with the catechumen. In this instance, the catechumen's family was not available to help at the shelter, but on another occasion, the two families might work together.

The Rite describes a well-rounded formation for catechumens that includes catechesis, community, liturgical rites and apostolic works. These four ways of bringing to maturity "the dispositions manifested at their acceptance into the catechumenate" (#75) compose the fullness of catechumenal formation.

Catechesis During the Catechumenate: Liturgical Catechesis

Many longtime ministers of initiation believe that the "suitable catechesis" described in the Rite should be a type of liturgical catechesis. I strongly believe that liturgical catechesis is the form of catechesis to be used for the period of the catechumenate.

Lectionary-based Catechesis

Liturgical catechesis has two primary elements: word and symbol. Catechesis that has lectionary readings as its point of departure has been called "lectionary-based catechesis," and it is part of the larger liturgical catechesis. The lectionary readings are the starting point for reflection on God's word and for a subsequent extended catechesis.

Lectionary-based catechesis fits the vision of formation in the Rite (#75) for it is "gradual and complete in its coverage." As catechumens and candidates gather around the word week after week, month after month, possibly even year after year, the liturgical cycle provides a catechesis that naturally flows with the life of the Church. In the *Constitution on the Sacred Liturgy*, the Second Vatican Council declared that "within the cycle of a year, moreover, the church unfolds the whole mystery of Christ, from his incarnation and birth until his ascension, but also as reflected in the day of Pentecost, and the expectation of blessed hope and of the Lord's return."[3] Certainly, unfolding the mystery of Christ is a complete catechesis for young catechumens.

Since lectionary-based catechesis is rooted in the liturgical year and flows from the Sunday Liturgy of the Word, it further fits the vision of the Rite that calls for catechesis to be "accommodated to the liturgical year, and solidly supported by celebrations of the word." Moreover, lectionary-based catechesis fulfills paragraph 75.3 in that it allows for the children to be "kindly dismissed" from the Liturgy of the Word and go forth for further reflection.

For you who are wondering if lectionary-based catechesis is "enough," the answer depends on what you mean by "enough." Since initiation is a process of conversion and not a religious education program, the lectionary seems to be one of the best instruments for leading catechumens to initiation. When following the lectionary, the whole mystery of Christ is unfolded and that should certainly be "enough" for initiation. In addition, the central Christian doctrines also flow from the lectionary readings. In the catechetical session that follows the breaking open of the word, doctrine is handed on to the catechumens and candidates. The doctrine easily flows with the cycle of the year. Rather than being scheduled in an academic syllabus, doctrine emerges as the mystery of Christ unfolds in the lectionary. Pope Paul VI said that the lectionary is the chief instrument for handing down Christian doctrine, and the center of all theological study.[4]

What does lectionary-based catechesis "look like"? Let me describe it for you.

Sample Session

Breaking Open the Word With Child Catechumens

"If we just try to be like Mary, we'll be closer to God." *Jessica, age seven (Fourth Sunday of Advent, Luke 1:26-38)*

"I had a friend who had an abortion. She has never smiled again." *Kimberly, age thirteen (Fourth Sunday of Advent, Matthew 1:18-24)*

"I argue a lot with my mom. I don't really know why." *Brad, age twelve (Seventh Sunday of the Year, Mark 2:1-12)*

"I imagine that Jesus went to a shabby little hut and had supper with some poor people." *Drew, age ten (Palm Sunday, Luke 22:14-23, 56)*

Breaking open the word is a type of lectionary-based catechesis that helps catechumens reflect more deeply on the meaning of God's word in their young lives. The examples above illustrate how God's word connects with the life experiences of children. When given the opportunity, children think deeply about what God is saying to them in the Scriptures. Their active imaginations allow God's word to run freely through their hearts and minds. Breaking open the word after it is proclaimed in the liturgy gives children the opportunity to explore God's message.

Immediately after the Liturgy of the Word, catechumens and candidates are dismissed from the assembly with their catechist to break open the word. Dismissal from a eucharistic liturgy happens primarily on Sunday, but it can also occur anytime catechumens and candidates are present at Mass, including weekday celebrations of the Eucharist or Catholic school Masses.

Method for Breaking Open the Word

Here is the structure of breaking open the word that I have used. Please remember that breaking open the word should be a fluid process. What follows is not meant to be a rigid outline that must be followed precisely. In addition, the total time of breaking open the word is approximately thirty minutes: from dismissal after the homily to the time Mass ends. Each step outlined below, therefore, takes a relatively short time to complete.

- Liturgy of the Word
- Dismissal of Catechumens and Candidates
- Gathering of Catechumens, Candidates and Catechist
- Gathering Ritual
- Proclamation of the Word
- Silence
- Initial Question
- Children's Response
- Simple Exegesis (explanation or analysis of the Scriptures)
- (Proclamation of the Word)
- Deeper Question by Catechist
- Children's Response
- Closing Ritual

Liturgy of the Word

The child catechumens and candidates celebrate the Liturgy of the Word as usual. Their family members, companions and sponsoring families are also present, if possible. Following the homily, the child catechumens and candidates are dismissed from the assembly. Family members who are practicing Catholics would remain in church for the celebration of the Eucharist. Parents who are catechumens or uncatechized candidates themselves might also be dismissed with the children.

Children's Liturgy of the Word

Some parishes dismiss all young children

after the opening prayer for a children's Liturgy of the Word. The children gather in a separate place for the Liturgy of the Word and return to the main assembly during the preparation of the gifts. If this is the case, the children who are catechumens and candidates could join their peers for the children's Liturgy of the Word. When the baptized children return to the main assembly, the catechumens and candidates meet their catechist for breaking open the word. Or, child catechumens and candidates may stay with the main assembly and be dismissed when adult catechumens and uncatechized candidates are dismissed.

Dismissal of Catechumens and Candidates

After the homily, the presider kindly dismisses the catechumens and uncatechized candidates, children and adults. The children's catechist and the adults' catechist come forward to receive the lectionary from the presider. The catechumens and uncatechized candidates process out of church with their catechists.

In some parishes, only catechumens are dismissed, while baptized candidates remain with the assembly. The rationale behind this option is that since candidates are baptized, they remain with the faithful, similar to baptized children who do not yet receive Eucharist remaining with their families. Baptized adult candidates—even if not catechized—have a right to remain for the Liturgy of the Eucharist even though they cannot receive Communion.

Gathering of Catechumens, Candidates and Catechist

Generally, the children meet with a catechist and the adults meet with a catechist. If the number and ages of the children warrant, there may be one catechist to meet with older children and one catechist to meet

with younger children. Companions may also meet with the catechumens and candidates on a regular or occasional basis. Also, there may be times when adults and children meet together for breaking open the word, especially if parents and children from the same family are candidates for initiation. Another option is for the sponsors or companions to meet with the children.

The place where the catechumens and candidates (technically known as the *catechumeneon*) meet with their catechist to break open the word has a connection to the worshiping assembly. Though the spaces do not need to be physically connected, the environment of the catechumeneon should be reminiscent of the worship space from which the catechumens and candidates have just been dismissed. The faithful participate in the Liturgy of the Eucharist while the catechumens and candidates participate in liturgical catechesis. The catechist enthrones the lectionary in a prominent place as she or he enters. The correct liturgical color is visible to indicate the season of the year. Candles may also be part of an enthronement. Comfortable chairs arranged in a circle encourage a shared reflection on the word.

Gathering Ritual

As the children enter and reverently take their places, the catechist enthrones the lectionary in the middle of the circle or in some other prominent place. Next, a simple weekly ritual needs to be established by the catechist as a way of helping the children to settle in the new space and feel comfortable with what is going to happen each week.

I have the children sit quietly as I light the candles. (Having children light the candles is dangerous and makes the lighting task more momentous than it is). Then, with hands outstretched, I pray an opening prayer grounded in the readings of the day. After this respectful tone has been set, I more casually welcome the children and give a brief introduction to the reflection of the day. I may ask them to listen for something specific in the reading. In some way I help them focus on the reading that they are about to hear again.

Sample Session

For the sake of this example, the readings are taken from the Mass for the Epiphany of the Lord (Isaiah 60:1-6; Psalm 72; Ephesians 3:2-3, 5-6; Matthew 2:1-12).

Catechist prays the opening prayer.

Catechist: Let us pray.

> God of glory,
> Your light has come into the world.
> Help us recognize your presence in our
>   lives.
> We ask this through Christ our Lord.

Children: Amen.

Catechist: Today is the feast of the Epiphany. Who remembers what Father said epiphany means? *(Children respond.)* Epiphany is the day of appearance. The Church celebrates God's "appearing" to us. God became human. God came to earth as the baby Jesus. Now God was a human that we could feel and touch and see. This was a sign of God's great love for us.

The story of the Epiphany is an action-packed story! There are lots of characters in the story. Listen carefully and I'll ask you to tell me who all the characters are. The characters have important messages for us.

Proclamation of the Word

Using the enthroned lectionary, the catechist proclaims the reading that is to be the focus of the reflection. I find that with children, one reading is usually sufficient for the proclamation and reflection. Children have an easier time listening to and focusing on one reading since such a short time (approximately thirty minutes) is involved. I usually use the Gospel because of its preeminence in the Liturgy of the Word. There are times, however, when using one of the other readings, or two or three of the readings helps illustrate a point or make a connection.

Proclaim Matthew 2:1-12.

Silence

A good amount of silence gives the children time to ponder the reading. It also heightens the sense of the importance of the reading.

Initial Question

After an ample time of silence, ask an initial question that is broad enough to allow for a range of responses. Don't make the question so narrow or specific that you stifle a divergent idea that one of the children might have. On the other hand, a question that is too general will leave the children without a sense of direction. If you suggested an idea in the introduction, that same idea should be used in the initial question.

My experience has shown me that children need a focused question. When breaking open the word with adults, the catechist might ask, "What struck you about the reading?" Or, "What did you hear in the reading?" Or, "What is your initial response to the reading?"

When children are asked general questions like these, they may be unresponsive. The questions are too abstract and vague for a child, especially for a young child. Children respond more easily when a concrete question is asked. As you lead the children deeper into the meanings of the reading, you will be able to ask somewhat more abstract questions.

Different readings require different types of questions. Each question has to be "custom made" for the children present as well as for the reading.

Catechist: I asked you to listen for all the characters in the story. Who were the characters?

Children's Response

Allow children plenty of time to answer. When there is silence, if the catechist remains calm and comfortable in the quiet, children are comfortable, too. Although the sample question above is straightforward, rephrasing more difficult questions is sometimes necessary.

Children: The kings (magi, astrologers), King Herod, Mary, Jesus, Joseph.

Catechist: The reading said that Herod called in some people to ask them where the Messiah was born. Who did Herod call? *(Catechist may have to read a part of the reading again.)*

Children: The priests and scribes.

Catechist: Were there any other main "characters" or things that were important in the reading? It may not necessarily be a person.

Children: The star.

Catechist: Let's talk about why these people and things are important in the reading.

Simple Exegesis

The initial questions are designed to get the children into the readings and connecting with the characters. In this example, the upcoming questions will also focus on the characters. Thus, some explanation of the reading will help the children understand the characters

and enable them to enter better into the story. The explanation is two or three minutes of pertinent information about the story and the reflection. It is adapted to be developmentally appropriate for the children present. The explanation takes the form of a dialogue with the children in order to involve them. This step is critical for helping young Christians know how to read and interpret the Scriptures.

Catechist: King Herod is one of the first characters mentioned in the reading. He had been ruler of Judea for about thirty years—a long time! He was appointed by Rome. Rome was the controlling government. The people of Judea didn't have their own government. Herod was part of the foreign government that ruled the people of Judea. Do you know any examples of foreign governments ruling a country today? (Talk about the examples.)

Herod was an unpopular king because he was part of the foreign government that ruled. And he never let the people of Judea make their own decisions. Why would he be so worried about a newborn baby king?

Children respond.

Catechist: We see some other foreigners in the story. The astrologers are "from the east." When Scripture says "from the east" that means they were from far away. So, foreigners were the ones to find and come to baby Jesus. What message do you think God is trying to give us? *(Pause for children's response)*. God is telling us in this story that Jesus came for all people, including "foreigners." Jesus came not just to save the Jews, but to save all people.

The foreigners are the ones who see the star. Jesus is the savior of all people! God gives signs, or "stars," to tell people that Jesus is their savior. But, not everyone sees the "stars," or the signs, that point the way to Jesus. The astrologers saw the star and believed that they would find the newborn king if they followed the star. Some people ignore the "stars," or signs, in their lives. Other people want to find God, and they pay attention to God's signs in their lives.

Deeper Question by the Catechist

The explanation flows into the deeper question by the catechist. Depending on the catechist's style, she or he may want to intertwine some of the explanation with questions as in these examples.

Catechist: What are signs in your life that God is present?

Children's Response

You should encourage each child to respond at some point during the discussion. Please be aware that there is a delicate balance between encouraging and pressuring a child to share. Be aware of nonverbal cues from the individual child. Speaking to the reluctant child after a session to learn how she or he feels about speaking in the group can also help.

Catechist: The first people to see the star were foreigners, and the people of Jesus' time considered them to be outcasts—people that other people didn't have anything to do with. Foreigners were considered untrustworthy. But, God appeared to them first. What message do you think God is trying to tell us in this story?

Children respond.

Catechist: If God were to appear first to foreigners, or "outcasts," in our country today, who would they be?

Children respond.

Closing Ritual

If an extended catechesis does not follow the breaking open of the word, then you should close the breaking open the word at the approximate time that Mass would be ending. Children then join their parents and sponsors after Mass, possibly for doughnuts and juice.

To conclude the breaking open of the word, summarize what has been said and close the session with a blessing of the catechumens (#95-97).

Catechist: The reading today tells us how God "appears" to us in our daily lives. God appears in ordinary ways, and sometimes God gives special signs, like the star. We have to be open and willing to see God's signs in our lives. Often God chooses to appear to the most unlikely people.

Blessing: Children, please stand.

(With hands outstretched over the children, the catechist prays from the ritual text. The text will need to be adapted if baptized candidates are present and are included in the blessing.)

Let us pray.

> God of power,
> look upon these your children
> as they deepen their understanding of the
>   Gospel.
> Grant that they may come to know and
>   love you
> and always heed your will
> with receptive minds and generous hearts.
> Teach them through this time of
>   preparation
> and enfold them within your church,
> so that they may share your holy mysteries
> both on earth and in heaven.
> We ask this through Christ our Lord.
> Amen.
> *(#97.C, slightly adapted)*

The catechist then goes to each child and lays hands on each one. This ends the session.

Break before the family catechetical session

When extended catechesis is to follow the breaking open of the word, summarize the session and invite the children to take a break while their parents, sponsors, sponsoring families and companions come from Mass to join the group.

Extended Family-centered Catechesis

Lectionary-based catechesis continues after the breaking open of the word with extended family-centered catechesis. In other words, the catechetical session that follows continues to flow from the readings of the day. The thoughts, reflections, ideas and questions raised by the children in the breaking open of the word are further explored in the catechetical session in which families, sponsors and companions participate.

The needs and questions of the children will influence how the doctrine flows from the lectionary readings. Often, more than one doctrinal issue emerges from the readings. Thus, you will need to be well-prepared and flexible during a session. The total time of the session would be approximately one to one and one-half hours; however, the sessions are meant to be fluid and flexible.

- Gathering
- Transition From Breaking Open the Word
- Proclamation of the Word
- Silence
- Word Leads Into Doctrine, Tradition, History (My Story and the Church's Story)
- Connecting My Story to the Church's Story
- Response
- Closing Ritual

Gathering

Breaking open the word ends about the same time Mass ends. Children take a break from their reflection on the word and meet their parents and sponsors after Mass. If parishioners are meeting for juice, coffee and doughnuts, then the families would join them. After a sufficient amount of time, the children, their families and the sponsoring families meet again to continue the lectionary-based catechesis.

Transition From Breaking Open the Word

Since the children have already broken open the word, the adults, siblings and companions who have joined them need to be "brought on board." Without repeating the reflection for those who have joined, you or one of the children should make the transition from the breaking open the word to the present moment.

Catechist: During our reflection this morning, we talked about how God "appears" to us. The feast of Epiphany celebrates God's "appearing" or coming to us as a human person. The star was a sign that God had "appeared" and that the Savior had been born. We talked about signs of God's presence in our lives. *(To the children)* Will someone tell the group what some of those signs were?

Children recount some of the stories of God's presence in their lives.

Catechist: The astrologers from the east saw the star and followed it to Jesus. Why is it important that people from the east saw the star?

Catechist: Let's focus again on God's word.

Proclamation of the Word

The Gospel is proclaimed once again. Or, if one of the other readings is to be discussed, it also may be proclaimed.

Silence

Word Leads Into Doctrine, Tradition, History

With the introduction given and the word as the foundation, you should now invite the group to explore the doctrinal implications of the reading. Or, depending on the reading and the questions that arise, the group may want to examine a historical question or a church tradition that surrounds the reading. For example, on Epiphany, some children want to explore the history of the magi and the stories that surround them. Another option is to spend more time on the explanation of the text and the meaning of the Epiphany. In the sample session given here, the discussion moves into a deeper consideration of the signs God gives, particularly the sacraments.

Catechist: In the reading, the star is mentioned four times. The author of Matthew's Gospel wanted to emphasize the star and its significance. Almost everyone knows the story of the great star in the sky at Christmas. We see it in pictures and on Christmas cards. But, the reason it is so important is not the star itself or its astrological significance. It is important because it pointed to something more. It pointed to Jesus, the Son of God. The star pointed to something more than itself,

something greater. It pointed to God's presence on earth in the person of the baby Jesus.

Earlier this morning, the catechumens and candidates talked about signs in their lives. They described signs in their lives that tell them God is present. Signs of God's presence are not usually big, awesome things like the star. They are often small like... *(name signs of God that the children identified earlier).*

(My Story) Small-group Work

Divide the group into random groups of children and adults.

Catechist: The catechumens and candidates spoke of signs of God's presence in their lives. Parents, sponsors and friends, I'd like you to take a moment to describe to the catechumens and candidates in your group a sign of God's presence in your life.

After the small group discussion, bring the group back together for some doctrinal input.

(Church's Story) Catechesis on the Meaning of Sacrament

- The Church has special signs in its life: the seven sacraments.
- A sacrament is a visible sign of God's presence.
- Ordinary things point to God's presence. *(During the break, the catechist adds two or three of the primary symbols to the enthronement that holds the lectionary: water, oil, bread and wine.)*
- The sacraments are different from signs like the star. In the sacraments, God actually is present.
- Christians believe that sacraments "give grace." Grace is God's presence. The sacraments make God present in a special way.
- Sacraments are also celebrations. They celebrate God's presence and action in our lives.
- We celebrate the actions of:

— Creating new life (Baptism)
— Welcoming persons into a new community (Baptism, Confirmation, Eucharist)
— Sharing a meal (Eucharist)
— Forgiving and healing (Reconciliation and Anointing of the Sick)
— Commitment (Marriage, Holy Orders)

Connecting My Story to the Church's Story

Now invite the group to connect their story to the Church's story. Ask how the Church's teaching or tradition connects with their own experience.

Catechist: I'd like each of you to choose one of the actions that we just described. Choose something that you have experienced in your family. For example, you recently welcomed a new baby sister, brother, niece or nephew; you joined the soccer team; you had a special meal to celebrate good grades. Answer these questions about the event:

■ What made the event or action special?
■ Who was present?
■ What did you do to celebrate?

Allow time for each family to talk among themselves and with their sponsoring family. Or, use the small-group combinations that were used earlier. Small groups share their response to the first question with the larger group. Then summarize by making connections back to the Church's story.

Response

Ask a final question that will help the children turn outward with a response to God's word and Church teaching and tradition.

Catechist: We have talked about many different signs that God gives us. There are signs of God's everyday presence in our lives and there are also special signs in the Church called

sacraments. What do we need to do to be aware of the signs of God's presence in our lives?

Parents talk with their children about this question, or sponsors talk with the children.

Closing Ritual

Paragraph 96 of the Rite calls for a blessing to be given at the end of a celebration of the word and at "the end of a meeting for catechesis." The blessing includes a simple prayer and the laying on of hands by the catechist, priest or deacon who does the blessing. Parents may also lay hands on their children.

I recommend doing this every week after each catechetical session. In this way, the blessing becomes a weekly ritual. Exorcisms (#90-94) and anointings (#98-103) may also be used (see section on "Minor Rites," pages 80-82). Other types of prayer may also be used to close the session. Prayers will need to be adapted for your particular mix of catechumens and candidates. The prayer below is only a sample adaptation.

Catechist: Everyone please stand for the closing blessing. Those of you who are baptized please extend your hands with me over the catechumens and candidates.

(Catechist says or sings) Let us pray.

> Lord,
> form these catechumens and candidates by the mysteries of the faith,
> that they may be brought to rebirth in baptism, strengthened in Confirmation and nourished in the Eucharist,
> May they be counted among the members of your church.
> We ask this through Christ our Lord.
> Amen.
> *(#97. A, adapted)*

Catechist should then lay hands on each child.
Baptized parents and sponsors may also lay hands
on their children.

Catechist: Go in peace.

Summary of Lectionary-based Catechesis

The Liturgy of the Word, the breaking open of the word and extended family-centered catechesis together form lectionary-based catechesis and make it a pivotal part of formation during the period of the catechumenate. These three components would fit together on a Sunday morning as follows:

9-9:30 a.m. Liturgy of the Word (Catechumens and candidates with assembly)
9:30-10 a.m. Breaking open the word (Catechumens and candidate with catechist)
10-10:15 a.m. Break
10:15-11:15 a.m. Extended catechesis (Parents, siblings, sponsors, sponsoring families and companions join catechumens and candidates after Mass.)

Option: Companions and sponsors may join catechumens and candidates for breaking open the word.

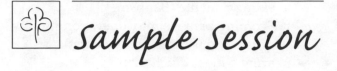

Catechist Preparation for Lectionary-based Catechesis

One of the most important elements for successful catechumenate catechesis is your preparation as a catechist. Prayerful, thorough, thoughtful preparation is essential. As anyone who works with children knows, "winging it" leads to frustration on the part of both the children and the catechist. The steps described below will help you prepare for the breaking open the word and the extended catechesis that follows. If two different catechists do the two parts, they should prepare the overall session together.

The preparation is based on the lectionary readings of the day. There are three parts to the preparation and each part has several steps.

Part One is for the catechist. The catechist reflects personally upon the readings as a follower of Jesus Christ. In order to lead the children into a discovery of the meaning of the word in their lives, the catechist must have explored the readings and their meaning for his or her own life.

Part Two is the preparation for the children. Once the word has taken root in the catechist's heart, the focus is on the children and how they will hear and respond to the word.

Part Three is the preparation for the extended catechesis. Having wrestled with the word, the catechist now considers the questions, issues and doctrine that the readings raise.

Part One: Personal Preparation

1. Pray. Begin by praying for openness and guidance from the Spirit. Pray for each catechumen and candidate.

2. Read the readings silently. Read all the readings, including the psalm. Read them slowly and deliberately.

3. Sit silently. Really listen. Let the word roam randomly within you.

4. Read the readings again.

5. Write. Write the words, phrases, images from the text that strike you.

6. Write feelings. Write down any feelings that you experienced as you read or reflected on the readings.

7. Read the readings aloud.

8. Consult commentaries on the text. Once you have spent time with the readings, then read at least one or two commentaries on the texts. Reading the commentaries too early tends to bias one's way of thinking about the readings. Once you have done the initial reflection for yourself, then consult another source. Make note of any insights you gain from the commentaries. Reading the Scripture commentaries will also help you prepare to explain the readings during the breaking open of the word.

   To do this preparation, you will need copies of commentaries that you can easily use at home. While *The New Jerome Biblical Commentary* may be useful, most catechists do not have their own copy, nor do they have time to go to the parish library to read it. Simple commentaries like the ones found in *At Home with the Word* by Liturgy Training Publications are helpful and easy to use.

9. Ask yourself, "What is the message of the readings for me?" Begin to focus on the central word, image or message the readings have for you. Read the readings again. Let the readings take hold of you.

Part Two: Preparation for the Children

1. Think of the catechumens and candidates. Pray for them.

2. Read the readings with the ear of a child. Listen for the words, images and characters that would speak to a child. Ask yourself, "What would the children hear in these readings?" "How would a child feel about these readings?" "What questions might a child have?" Consider what would catch the attention of children. Children, especially younger ones, are attracted to more concrete images: storms at sea, a man with a withered hand, a woman searching for a coin, a child who is sick, a farmer and a vineyard. Children can also focus rather easily on the person of Jesus. By this time they know who Jesus is. They can picture him and what he is doing and saying.

3. Consult lectionary-based materials for children. What insights do these resources provide? As with Scripture commentaries, lectionary-based materials for children provide good background information. These materials help you consider aspects of the readings you might have missed or not even considered. Consulting other sources helps to ensure that you are not just giving your own interpretation of the Scriptures. Also, the lectionary-based materials give ideas for framing questions for children. Some of the materials provide helpful explanatory information in a way that is interesting and understandable for children.

   I consult several lectionary-based

resources for children to help me think about the readings and then to help me design the catechetical session. The lectionary-based materials give good suggestions for sessions as well as insight into the readings. I take ideas from different sources to design a session that fits the catechumens and candidates. Some helpful lectionary-based materials are: *Living the Good News* (Living the Good News, Inc.), *Seasons of Faith* (BROWN-ROA), *Sunday* (Treehaus Communications, Inc.), *Celebrating the Lectionary* (Resource Publications, Inc.).

4. Determine what questions you will ask the children and how you will guide the reflection. Once you have done some serious reflection and study of the readings, you are ready to decide in what direction you will lead the discussion. Decide where you are headed with the reflection and then determine the questions or other method you will use with the children. The initial question starts to point the children in a direction, but leaves room for the children to take another direction if they wish. The initial question is meant to get the children into the story and thinking about what is happening. Questions that focus on the characters or on a specific phrase or image are often effective for drawing children into the story. The Epiphany sample session dealt with a question about the characters. For other readings, initial questions might be:

■ How do you think Jesus felt when all those people kept following him?
■ Why do you think Jesus worked his first miracle at a wedding?
■ Why were the disciples trying to keep little children away from Jesus?
■ Jesus used the word *hypocrite*. What is a hypocrite?

After determining the opening question that leads the children into the story, decide how you will lead into the explanation that follows. The initial question leads into the simple exegesis. Or, if the children take the discussion in a direction other than the one you intended, you need to be prepared and flexible enough to go with the children's lead. If you have spent time with the readings and prepared well, even though the children go in a different direction, your familiarity with the readings will allow you to flow with the children.

The brief exegesis comes from the commentaries and lectionary-based materials that you consulted. These sources give information that will help you and the children better understand the readings. The children might need to know something about the culture and history of Jesus' time. Or, they might need to know about the author's intended audience and why a particular story is told the way it is. They might need to know what a parable is and how Jesus used them. Or, they might need some background on miracle stories or healing stories. A small amount of information will help the children understand the Scripture and not burden or bore them with unnecessary information. The explanation helps the children understand the reading so that they more easily apply the message to their own lives.

The explanatory piece also helps draw the children more deeply into the story. It leads to the next level of questioning. The deeper questions are more pointed and directed. They help the children name the message of the story. Eventually, the second question, or set of questions, leads to the extended catechesis that follows the breaking open of the word.

Instead of using a question-and-answer format, another option is to lead the children in a guided meditation on the gospel. Some stories lend themselves easily to this method of reflection.

Ask the children to relax and quiet themselves. Then, invite the children to use their imaginations as you use guided imagery to lead them through a meditation on the Gospel. After the meditation, ask the children to describe how characters in the story might have felt or how they themselves felt being "in the story" with Jesus. Then, the catechist moves to the deeper questions that get at the meaning of the story.

5. Prepare the opening and closing prayers. Determine how you will open and close the breaking open the word. If extended catechesis is to follow, the closing ritual would follow the catechetical session.

6. Prepare for questions that may arise. At times you can predict questions that children will raise about the readings. If possible, think about your response in advance.

Part Three: Preparation for Extended Family-centered Catechesis

1. List the themes, issues and questions that came out of the readings. Based on the season of the liturgical year, the prayer, study and reflection you have done and the needs of the catechumens, candidates and their families, write down themes, issues and questions that come from the readings. Generally, there will be one or two dominant themes or issues that emerge. Some will be more appropriate and will "fit" better with the needs of the children and their families.

2. Determine the catechetical direction. Knowing the children and their families and seeing the issues and questions that arise

from the readings, determine what theme, issue or question needs more attention. More time may need to be spent on the scriptural explanation and interpretation. The possibilities for catechesis on doctrine are as deep and rich as the Scriptures themselves. Once again, the readings and the needs of the children determine the content rather than a parish syllabus.

3. Prepare appropriate family-centered catechesis. Plan the way in which the children and their families will gather again after breaking open the word. Or, if the session is at a time other than immediately following Mass, plan a gathering ritual. Prepare the catechetical session using appropriate catechetical techniques for intergenerational sessions.

Small-group Activities

A family-based catechetical session is an intergenerational session in which families and individuals participate. A variety of creative and nontraditional activities can be included. Family-centered catechesis does not mean that every discussion and activity has to be a family activity. At times, you should group children according to their ages; at other times, have a catechumenal family and a sponsoring family meet together; or form groups with diverse ages or composed of members from different families. An added advantage is that when parents and children are together in a session, you have little worry about discipline.

Small groups meet for a discussion or activity and then come together for large group sharing.

Pairing

Another session might include time for a catechumen or candidate to pair off with a child from a sponsoring family. For example, two (or three) children work on their description of Jesus. They can use words, paint, paper, string, pictures, music, clay or whatever they choose to describe Jesus. Meanwhile, the parent of a catechumen or candidate pairs with a parent from the sponsoring family to talk about how they perceived Jesus as a child and how they see Jesus today. Or, an older child from a sponsoring family pairs with a young catechumen to help with an activity or discussion. I often use pairing for "Walk-and-Talk" time. Pairs are given a question, a reading or a story and are asked to "take a walk" and talk about the question or reading. (The freedom to remain silent is always an option.) Pairing can be done in any combination and can be used in a variety of situations.

Lastly, even though creative techniques and fun projects for families are enjoyable and helpful, the emphasis always remains on God's word. Avoid using cute projects or crafts to fill time. Although "hands-on" activities are good for children, be sure they always have a clear purpose. Other types of intergenerational activities that get children involved but are not necessarily "craft projects" are:

- brainstorming;
- role-playing;
- create-a-print (use newsprint or poster to create a story or depict an idea);
- storytelling;
- baking bread or making a meal;
- nature walks.

Feel free to use effective methods frequently if they are focused on the word. The purpose of family-centered catechesis during the catechumenate is to help families focus on God's word and apply the Church's story to their own lives. As long as the word is central and the catechist is well-prepared, families do not need weekly gimmicks to keep their attention.

4. Read the readings and assess your faithfulness to the word. When the preparation of the catechetical session is complete, return to the readings and read them again. Ask yourself if you have been faithful to the word. Does the word of God remain prominent? Review the flow from the breaking open the word through the extended catechesis. If anything is forced or contrived, make adjustments where needed.

5. Prepare the closing ritual. According to the season of the year and the needs of the catechumens and candidates, determine what blessing or minor exorcism will be celebrated at the end of the session (#90-103). If a priest or deacon is available for a session, an anointing can be used. Another type of closing prayer may also be used. Prepare the prayers and music that will be needed. Practice presiding if you are a novice at this.

Lastly, the preparation process outlined here suggests ways to prepare the breaking open the word with children and the extended catechesis that follows. You will find that, as you become more comfortable and experienced with the process, the steps will smoothly flow together. What may seem like a lengthy, multistep process will become a natural progression for sharing God's word with young catechumens, candidates and their families.

Summary of Lectionary-based Catechesis During the Catechumenate

Lectionary-based catechesis is part of the larger process of liturgical catechesis and is a primary means of formation during the entire catechumenate process. Lectionary-based catechesis during the period of the catechumenate is based on the Liturgy of the Word. The Liturgy of the Word is followed by the breaking open of the word and then an extended catechesis that is family-centered. Preferably, the entire process takes place on Sunday morning, although the extended catechesis portion could take place at another time.

A Sunday morning session might look like this:

9 a.m. Liturgy of the Word
9:30 a.m. Dismissal of catechumens and candidates
9:35 a.m. Breaking Open the Word
— Re-gathering of Catechumens, Candidates With Catechist
— Gathering Ritual
— Proclamation of the Word
— Silence
— Initial Question
— Children's Response
— Simple Exegesis
— (Proclamation of the Word)
— Deeper Question by the Catechist
— Children's Response
10 a.m. Break
10:15 a.m. Extended Catechesis
— Gathering of Catechumens, Candidates, Parents, Siblings, Sponsoring Families or Sponsors and Companions
— Transition From Breaking Open the Word to the Catechetical Session
— Proclamation of the Word
— Silence

— Word Leads Into Doctrine, Tradition, History (My Story and Church's Story)
— Connecting My Story to the Church's Story
— Response
11:15 a.m. Closing Ritual

Thus, the entire process is grounded in the Liturgy of the Word and takes place on Sunday when the assembly is gathered for worship. The catechumens, candidates and their families are formed by the word, the liturgy and the assembly.

Sacramental Catechesis

Many people ask, "When you use lectionary-based catechesis in the catechumenate, when are the children prepared for the sacraments?"

The entire process of conversion prepares, or better yet, leads children to the sacraments. Initiation is not a sacramental preparation program. Sacramental preparation in most parishes primarily teaches children and parents about a sacrament and prepares them to celebrate that sacrament. It includes workbooks, classes, meetings and assignments. This type of sacramental preparation does not generally fit the vision of initiation, which fundamentally has to do with leading people to the paschal mystery.

Nevertheless, the journey of Christian initiation does culminate in the celebration of the sacraments. Leading children to celebrate the most sacred Christian mysteries is the climax of the journey. But, leading children to mystery cannot be accomplished through programs and textbooks. Children are led to mystery by word and symbol. The previous section on lectionary-based catechesis described how God's word is key in the initiation process. The prayers of the various liturgies are also part of the "word" that leads to mystery. Praying with and breaking open the prayers and blessings of the rites are also part of the complete process of liturgical catechesis.

Using liturgical symbols to "prepare" or lead to the ultimate celebration of the sacraments is known as sacramental catechesis.[6] Sacramental catechesis is part of liturgical catechesis. It is based upon a primary symbol of the sacrament, whereas lectionary-based catechesis is based upon the word proclaimed in the liturgy.

Sacramental catechesis may be included as part of the formation process of the period of the catechumenate. Family-centered catechetical sessions may be a time for sacramental catechesis. For example, some years the Church celebrates the Baptism of the Lord on the Sunday after Epiphany. The readings for the Baptism of the Lord could lead into a catechetical session in which the symbol of water is "broken open." In addition, the readings for the Eleventh Sunday of the Year (Cycle C) have powerful images of anointing. The extended catechesis for this week could be a breaking open of the symbol of oil and exploring the meaning of the Sacrament of Confirmation. There are many Sundays in which the readings contain strong eucharistic images (Seventeenth, Eighteenth, Nineteenth Sundays of Cycle B; Twenty-eighth Sunday of Cycle A; Corpus Christi). On these occasions, the symbol of bread could be broken open as a way of leading into the mystery of the Eucharist.

A session of sacramental catechesis may also follow one of the celebrations of the word that are "held specially for the catechumens" (#81). Or, some catechumens and candidates may ask for time to focus singularly on the Eucharist. If this is the case, there could be a session of sacramental catechesis that is designed specifically for the needs or questions of the children and their families. A session like this might be independent of the Sunday readings, yet still lead the children to the upcoming celebration of the sacrament.

According to Linda Gaupin, there are four aspects of a sacramental symbol to be "cracked open":

■ the human experience;
■ the biblical experience;
■ the ecclesial experience;
■ the ritual experience.

The human experiences of the symbol are the ordinary and extraordinary ways that the children, and other people, encounter the symbol in their lives. For example, baking, eating, smelling, kneading, needing, wheat, dinner, pitas, tortillas, bagels and Wonder Bread are all part of the human experience of bread.

The biblical experience of the symbol is the scriptural foundation of the symbol. For example, bread is seen in the Scriptures as manna in the desert, as loaves shared by a boy and in a meal shared by Jesus.

The ecclesial experience of the symbol is what the Church says about the meaning of the symbol. For example, the Church believes that eucharistic bread is the Body of Christ and that the bread is to be shared.

The ritual experience of the symbol is the place the symbol has in the ritual life of the Church. For example, bread is ritually broken and shared in the community.

Examining the four aspects of the symbol helps plumb the depth of meaning in the sacrament. Talking to children about the mystery of death-resurrection celebrated in baptism is flat and ineffective compared to letting their minds, hearts and bodies imagine the destructive, life-giving power of rushing, gushing real water. By asking children to delve into various aspects of water, oil, light or bread, they unpack for themselves the meaning of sacrament.

Sample Session

A Sample Sacramental Catechesis on Water

Here is a session that breaks open the symbol of water. [7] The structure is straightforward. Start with the human experience, move to the biblical and ecclesial experience and make the connections with the children's experience, and then celebrate with ritual. An outline of the session looks like this:

- Gathering
- Human Experience of the Symbol
  (Imaginative Exercise on Human Experience of the Symbol)
- Biblical Experience of the Symbol
  (Connect the Human Experience to Scripture)
- Ecclesial Experience of the Symbol
  (Connect Human Experience and Scripture to the Church's Experience of the Symbol)
- Ritual Experience of the Symbol
  (Celebrate With a Ritual Experience of the Symbol)

This example was designed for a session for the feast of the Baptism of the Lord. It is meant to follow the breaking open the word.

Gathering

After Mass parents, families and sponsoring families join the catechumens and candidates. If the session is independent of a Sunday liturgy, an appropriate welcome and gathering time would begin the session. An enthronement is already present when the session begins. The enthronement visually sets a focus for the session. The symbol that is the focus for the session is prominent in the room.

Once people have gathered, an opening prayer or song begins the session.

In the middle of the room, the lectionary is still enthroned from the breaking open of the word. In addition, there is a large, clear glass bowl full of water and glass pitchers full of water. The group gathers in chairs around the enthronement as the catechist welcomes them.

Opening song: "O Healing River" (Or, another song from the liturgy is used.)

The Human Experience

This movement helps the children, their families and sponsoring families reflect on the daily use and experience of water. The catechist designs an exercise that allows children and adults to recall ordinary and extraordinary realities of water. I often use a meditation or "focusing exercise" followed by time for brainstorming.

For the opening meditation and brainstorming exercise, the children and adults stay together in a large group.

Catechist: We heard in the readings this morning that Jesus was baptized in the Jordan River. I'm going to invite you to do some imagining with me. First, I will ask you to get relaxed. *(Lead the group in some deep breathing and relaxation exercises.)*

Next, I'd like you to imagine for a moment what the Jordan is like. Picture the water. Watch it flow. Feel the water. Picture the river bank. Feel the air around the water.

Just stand and watch the river for a while. *(Pause)*

Now, come back from the river.

I invite you to share aloud any word you associate with water.

Children and adults respond with words like: wet, cold, flowing, swimming, drenching, refreshing, cleansing....

Catechist: Now, I'd like you to move beyond the river and let your mind fill with images of any type of water.

The children and adults respond with more water images. The catechist may have to ask for the positive and the negative aspects of water. Examples of the kind of words and phrases that will emerge are: bath, rain, cooking, destructive, floods, growing plants, storms, hurricanes, ocean, lakes, streams, clouds, glass of water, steam, drowning, waves, lakes, ice, boiling, powerful, raging currents, water in the basement, beach, gutters, washing, soap, drink, thirst, water around the baby in the womb, mist, condensation....

The list goes on indefinitely. Encourage the group to think broadly and let the free association continue for some time. As the group says the words aloud, write all the words on newsprint to keep them visible.

Catechist: You have named many, many kinds of water, many uses for water, both positive and negative aspects of water. We see that there are many life-giving and creative uses for water, like cooking, bathing, cleansing, water for growing plants, drinking. We also named some negative, destructive aspects of water like floods, drowning, hurricanes. Water is good and is absolutely necessary for life, but it also can be powerful and deadly.

The Biblical Experience

You then move the discussion to the biblical stories about water. Stories from the Hebrew Scriptures and the Christian Scriptures are used. Use various techniques to explicate the Scriptures. One story may be told. Several stories may be compared. Or, another method may be used to unfold the biblical experience of the symbol.

Catechist: In the Scriptures we see a similar experience of water. We see stories where water is helpful, healing and good. We also see stories where water is destructive. I'd like you to work in your family/sponsor pairs to remember some of the scriptural stories you have heard that have water in them. Write

down a phrase that tells us what the story is. Secondly, how is the water used in the story? Is there a message in the water? Find the story in the Bible, if you can.

Give each family group a Bible. The catechumen's family works with the sponsoring family to make the list. Help groups as needed. Parents encourage children to remember stories.

When the families have finished, the large group reconvenes. After the families have told about the Scripture stories they remember, you should use the examples the families give to show that, in the Scriptures, water is a sign of life and freedom (Israelites and the Red Sea) as well as a sign of death and destruction (Egyptians and the Red Sea). The catechist also refers to the readings of the day. Stories that families have named include:

- Creation
- Noah and the ark
- Parting of the Red Sea
- Crossing the Jordan River to the promised land
- Jesus walking on water
- Jesus calming the storm
- Woman at the well
- Jesus changing water into wine at Cana

The Ecclesial Experience

Connect the human and biblical experiences of water to Church teachings on the meaning of water. Once again, various techniques may be used to share the Church's story of water.

Catechist: The Church also has its own story about water. In the early days of the Church, people were baptized much like Jesus was. After catechumens had been through a process of initiation, much like the one you are experiencing, they would be baptized in a river or maybe some other pool of water. The Church believed, and still believes today, that through the water, God cleanses the person and creates new life.

Return to the original brainstorming list the group created and connect what was given with what the Church believes about water. For example, ask the children to pick out all the words or phrases that relate to water being life-giving (words related to drinking, cooking, growing, etc.). You can then describe how the Church believes that water is a sign of new life.

The Ritual Experience

The fourth element of sacramental catechesis is the ritual experience of the symbol. A simple ritual can be a foretaste of the sacrament that is to come. It primes and prepares the children for the ultimate celebration of the sacramental ritual. The ritual experience of the symbol does not have to be the final step in the process of sacramental catechesis. The ritual may be the first step in the process.

Invite the group to shift to prayer posture. Music helps to change the tone of the session to a time of prayer. Approach the water and move it around with your hand. Then, lead the prayer.

Catechist: Let us stand and pray.

> God of life,
> through your holy prophets
> you proclaimed to all who draw near you,
> "Wash and be cleansed,"
> and through Christ you have granted us
>   rebirth in the Spirit.
> Bless these your children
> as they earnestly prepare for the
>   sacraments of initiation.
> Fulfill your promise:
> sanctify them in preparation for your gifts,
> that they may enter the community of your
>   Church.
> We ask this through Christ our Lord.
> Amen.
> *(#96.B, adapted)*

Invite the catechumens to come to the water.

Sprinkle or splash the child's hands, face and head with the water and invite the parent and sponsor to do the same. The prayer and ritual will need to be adapted if you have candidates as well as catechumens.

Closing Song: "O Healing River"

Using liturgical symbols to lead young catechumens to the meaning and mystery of the sacraments is a part of the "suitable catechesis" of the period of the catechumenate. Breaking open and looking into the meaning of a sacramental symbol reveals something about the nature of the sacrament.

Options for Catechesis During the Catechumenate

Liturgical catechesis is the model presented in this chapter for catechesis during the period of the catechumenate. The two forms of liturgical catechesis are lectionary-based catechesis (breaking open the word and the extended catechesis that follows) and occasional sacramental catechesis. All forms of catechesis are family-centered with the exception of the breaking open of the word. This, however, is not the only way that "suitable catechesis" can happen in the catechumenate.

The most important element of the catechumenate catechesis is the Sunday Liturgy of the Word with the dismissal of the catechumens and candidates for their weekly breaking open the word. This part is essential for remaining faithful to the vision of catechesis described in the Rite (#75). An option, however, might be to have the extended catechesis take place during the week rather than immediately following Mass on Sunday. Sometimes parents' work schedules prevent families from coming on Sunday morning. Or, sometimes children live with a different parent on weekends than they do during the week.

Furthermore, weekly gatherings of the entire family for an extended catechesis is too demanding for some family schedules. In these cases, children still meet every Sunday for the breaking open the word, whereas the entire family meets for the extended catechesis once or twice a month.

Children could also meet for extended catechesis while parents meet separately on various occasions for related adult-formation sessions. This may be advantageous if parents are returning Catholics with a lot of negative "baggage" that would cloud and clutter formation sessions for children. On the other hand, the negative aspect of this option is that the family is separated. Family-centered catechesis keeps the family together in a time in our culture when family-time is often limited. Separate sessions for adults and children do not allow for faith-sharing among the members of the family unless this is done at home after the session. Nevertheless, each parish needs to find a model that works best for its families.

In addition, including candidates in the regular catechetical program may work in some small parishes, especially those that use a lectionary-based approach. Also, candidates that are in a Catholic school receive some of their catechetical formation through the school. Remember, however, that inclusion in a religious education for the baptized is not the norm.

Celebrating the Minor Rites of the Catechumenate With Children

"Why is she doing that?" Andrea whispered to her mother, as I stretched out my hands and sang the prayer of blessing. Her mother politely quieted Andrea and smiled.

Andrea's question indicated that she was well aware that something about the blessing of catechumens was special. No longer was the moment catechetical; it had changed to a time of worship. The session ended on a prayerful, reverent and assuring tone.

The various "Rites Belonging to the Period of the Catechumenate" (#81-117) have been mentioned several times throughout this chapter. Although the celebration of the minor rites of the catechumenate is not mentioned in Part II of the Rite, once again, what is said in Part I applies to children as well. The "minor rites" as they are often called are liturgical rites celebrated during the period of the catechumenate. They are an important part of the formation of the catechumens. This section will discuss celebrations of the word of God, minor exorcisms, blessings of the catechumens, and anointing of the catechumens, particularly as they are celebrated as part of a "meeting for catechesis" (#92, 96) or "wherever this seems beneficial or desirable" (#98).

First, as part of a "meeting for catechesis" a qualified catechist may be the presiding celebrant for the exorcisms and blessings. The Rite does not specify who is the presider for the celebrations of the word. Presumably, a priest would preside at the Liturgy of the Word at the Sunday Mass, but a qualified catechist, deacon or priest could preside at the other celebrations of the word. The Rite describes a qualified catechist as one who has been "deputed by the bishop" for this ministry (#12, 16). In many dioceses, if a catechist is considered "qualified" by her or his pastor, that catechist is considered qualified by the bishop to preside at the appropriate minor rites. You should check with your pastor to determine if this is the case in your diocese.

Presiding at the exorcisms and blessings is an advantage because the children are usually most comfortable with their catechist, with whom they have spent a great deal of time; however, priests and deacons may also preside at any of the minor rites. I recommend that every catechetical session end with a blessing or exorcism.

Celebrations of the Word of God (#81-89)

A great deal has already been said about the primacy of God's word in the period of the catechumenate. In addition to participation in the Liturgy of the Word at the Sunday eucharistic celebration, celebrations of the word are to be held especially for the catechumens, and they can be held in connection with catechetical instruction.

Children would participate in any celebrations of the word held for adult catechumens and candidates. For example, during the slower, calmer days of summer, a parish may hold a celebration of the word of God for catechumens on Thursday evenings. Readings from Esther, Ruth or other books of the Bible that are not often heard in the regular lectionary cycle may be used. After the celebration of the word, hospitality time is offered to all. Or, as another example, catechetical sessions may be offered for catechumens and candidates at various times throughout the year. A celebration of the word of God would conclude or begin the catechesis.

Minor Exorcisms (#90-94)

Although some people wonder if minor exorcisms are necessary or appropriate for children, I believe that they are. The purpose of the minor exorcisms is not so much about sin and evil, as it is about living the "Christian life" and the "unending need for God's help." Certainly, children can benefit from these prayers as much as adults.

A minor exorcism is celebrated at the beginning or end of a meeting for catechesis. The rite is composed of a prayer said with outstretched hands. Although the Rite does not call for such an adaptation, the presider may also invite baptized parents to stretch out their hands over their children during the rite. Minor exorcisms can easily be the concluding rite of a catechetical session.

Minor exorcism can be used on several occasions. During the catechumenate at Our Lady of Good Counsel Parish, an exorcism was celebrated after one of the children "confessed" to the group that he had gotten in some serious trouble. And, an exorcism was celebrated after the Austin family had a family argument during one of the sessions. An exorcism might also be celebrated after a discussion on racism, sexism, war or some other societal evil.

Blessings of the Catechumens (#95-97)

The blessings of the catechumens "are a sign of God's love and of the Church's tender care." The structure of the rite is the same as that of the minor exorcism, except that the presider lays hands on the children after the prayer. Although the rite does not call for sponsors to lay hands on the candidates, I encourage baptized parents to lay their hands on their children after the catechist has completed the blessing.

Anointing of the Catechumens (#100)

The anointing of catechumens is also to be celebrated several times during the course of the catechumenate. The anointings ordinarily take place within a celebration of the word. As an adaptation, the anointing may conclude the breaking open of the word or the extended catechesis that flow from the Liturgy of the Word.

Like the adults, children would also frequently be anointed during the catechumenate. They relish the anointing. They are captivated by the feel of the greasy oil on their skin. They love to talk about being smeared with the oil and how it made them feel. In addition, parents feel a sense of reassurance knowing the Church lavishes such attention and concern on their children.

The presiding celebrant for the rite is a priest or deacon. The Oil of Catechumens is used to anoint the catechumens, and the anointing symbolizes their need for God's help and strength. Baptized candidates are not to be anointed, but they may receive a blessing.

Sample Session

Preparing for the Minor Rites

When preparing for the breaking open of the word and/or the extended catechesis that follows, decide which, if any, of the minor rites is best suited for the conclusion of the session. You may want to consult with the initiation coordinator when preparing for a minor rite. If you are presiding at the minor exorcism or blessing, you may want to practice presiding. The liturgist or initiation coordinator can work with you to develop presiding skills. If you are not comfortable presiding, however, or if you just don't have the skills for presiding, you should consult with the initiation coordinator who should find another catechist to preside. Please do not forgo celebrating the minor rites because you cannot preside.

As a catechist with little experience at presiding, I find that standing in front of a mirror and rehearsing helps me to do a better job. I also practice intoning any prayers or blessings I am going to sing (I am most definitely not a singer or cantor).[8] It is best to memorize opening and closing prayers and blessings. In this way, the catechist is not fumbling with a book and can make better eye contact with the children. The time and effort spent practicing presiding results in better ritual.

Blessing for the Third Sunday of Advent

Catechist: Please stand. Children, please step forward and stand in front of your parents and sponsors. I would ask all baptized parents and sponsors to extend your hands over the catechumens and candidates.

Let us pray. (*With outstretched hands, the catechist sings*)

> God of power,
> Your servant John the Baptist proclaimed
>   the coming of the Savior.
> Look with favor upon these families, as
>   they await your Son.
> Grant that during this time of preparation,
> they may learn your truth and follow in
>   the way of the gospel.
> Grant this through Christ our Lord,

who lives and reigns now and forever. Amen.
(Based on #97. C, adapted for Advent)

The catechist goes to each candidate and catechumen and lays hands on them. Baptized parents and sponsors do the same.

Catechist: Go in peace until we meet next week.

In summary, liturgical rites "purify the catechumens little by little and strengthen them with God's blessing" (#75.3). The minor rites of the catechumenate are a simple, yet meaningful, part of the children's catechumenal formation. With proper guidance, you can preside at these rites and enhance your weekly catechesis.

Conversion and the Child Catechumen

As the catechumens and candidates progress through the period of the catechumenate, signs of conversion (or its lack) will emerge. The signs or indicators of conversion in a child are sometimes clear and at other times subdued. Let's consider conversion in the child catechumen and see how we can discern conversion as we prepare for the Rite of Election.

The period of the catechumenate is a time for the catechumens' conversion to become strong, a process that might take several years. While the signs of a child's conversion may take some time to become manifest, children can and do experience conversion. Since the earliest days of the Church's catechumenal ministry, the Church has believed in the conversion process for children. Let's look at two historical precedents.

Conversion in Children

Throughout its history, the Church has asked young catechumens to undergo catechumenal formation and conversion. In the early Church, Tertullian claimed that children should come for Baptism "when they are growing up, when they are learning, when they are being taught what they are coming to: Let them be made Christian when they have become competent to know Christ."[9]

Tertullian's statement here suggests two elements in the children's catechumenal formation: that children have the competency and ability to know Christ and that children are not to be made Christians until they understand what it means to know Christ. "To know Christ" implies more than an intellectual understanding. Rather, "to know Christ" means that one understands Jesus' message, including the call to conversion and discipleship. According to Tertullian, children are among those called to conversion and discipleship.[10]

In the apostolic tradition, Hippolytus also speaks of the conversion of the heart and of one's life-style. When he refers to the initiation of children, he says that if "the children can speak for themselves, they shall do so...."[11] This indicates that the children can speak about a conversion of heart and life-style comparable to that of the adults who are questioned and who answer in a similar way.[12]

Dimensions of Conversion

Children in the time of Tertullian and Hippolytus, as well as children today, experience conversion in different ways. During the catechumenate, a child's heart and life can be changed in dramatic or subtle ways. Before leaving the period of the catechumenate and moving ahead to celebrate the Rite of Election, "the catechumens are expected to have undergone a conversion in mind and in action" (#120). There are many dimensions to conversion in mind and action. There are also many different ways to identify the dimensions of conversion. Here, I'll discuss four dimensions of conversion in order to illustrate what conversion may look like in the life of a child catechumen or candidate and her or his family.[13]

The Affective Dimension

Seven-year-old Alicia had been a catechumen at St. Margaret Parish for about eight months. Although she had come to Mass and participated in the breaking open of the word on an occasional basis, her parents, who claimed to be practicing Catholics, were rarely seen. Alicia's sponsor, her uncle, came to some of the family sessions with her.

The initiation team agreed that something was amiss. Alicia and her family were not committed to the process and were not showing signs of conversion. Thus, the team agreed that the director needed to talk with Alicia's parents.

With some hesitation, I asked Alicia's parents to meet with me. At that time, I asked Alicia's mother, Shannon, about their lack of participation and about Alicia's seemingly lukewarm commitment to the process. Furthermore, I noted that in a few weeks discernment for the Rite of Election would occur. The team had doubts about the Alicia's readiness for initiation. Then I frankly said I was concerned that I did not often see them in church.

Much to my surprise, Shannon's eyes immediately filled with tears. I was expecting a defensive explanation about why their participation had been minimal. Instead, Shannon said, "You're right, we haven't been coming. Please don't hold this against Alicia." Then, she went on to explain that she was caring for her sick mother and was overwhelmed with the responsibilities of caring for her daughter and her mother in addition to her other responsibilities at work, home and church. Furthermore, she expressed resentment and anger toward her brother, Alicia's sponsor, because he was not helping more with their mother.

In the end, Shannon and her brother reconciled a long history of problems. He became more of a caregiver for his sick mother. Alicia, Shannon and their family began to participate more fully in church and in the process of initiation. A burden had been lifted from the family and life began to change.

Affective conversion is a movement from blockage of feelings to the acceptance of, and ability to use, feelings.[14] In Alicia's family, Shannon was blocking feelings of being overwhelmed and feelings of anger toward her brother. Once she recognized and accepted those feelings, she was able to open herself to the Good News and the process of conversion. Shannon was able to use her feelings to express herself to her brother and eventually place her worries in the hands of God. When Shannon was free, Alicia was also free. Alicia gradually became more engaging. She spoke about her sick grandmother and how she felt "sad." She, too, began to recognize and accept some of the difficulties in the family and her feelings about those difficulties.

The story of Alicia and her family illustrates not only affective conversion but how conversion can affect an entire family.

Although Alicia was the catechumen, the process of being initiated into a caring, compassionate community that cared about her family had an impact on Alicia and the family. Alicia herself experienced affective conversion in the acceptance of feelings about her grandmother and how sometimes Grandma's being sick was "hard." Although no specific class, lesson or session was conducted on "accepting feelings" or "family hardships," the team's awareness of Alicia and her family, the pastoral "interview" and the family's overall focus on God's word combined to help foster the conversion process.

On the other hand, affective conversion may happen only in the child. Brad, mentioned at the beginning of this chapter, frequently reflected on the fact that he and his mother often argued. Throughout the many months of the catechumenate, Brad gradually softened his harsh words about his mother. He often saw Jesus' words applying to his relationship with his mother. He became more accepting of his mother and her boyfriend. (Although Brad's parents had been divorced for some time, his mother had recently begun dating.)

At the discernment interview, his mother also spoke of the change she had seen in Brad. She said that the initiation process had brought her and Brad closer. She said that he seemed less angry and more willing to "open up" to her. The catechumenal process played a role in Brad's movement from anger to acceptance.

Other children may have a less noticeable experience of affective conversion. Twelve-year-old Derek, a candidate at St. Margaret Parish, experienced affective conversion as moving from no particular feelings at all about God to a sure, solid conviction that God loved him. At the initial interview with Derek, when asked how he felt about God, Derek sheepishly replied, "I don't know." For many months Derek remained fairly quiet about most issues.

At the time of the discernment interview, Derek spoke convincingly about how he loved God because "God helps me and cares for me." Nothing identifiably dramatic happened in the catechumenate process for Derek, but conversion is not necessarily spectacular. Conversion often happens slowly and quietly.

Children cannot always articulate their experience of affective conversion since affective conversion is about one's feelings and emotions. Moral and social conversion can more easily be observed since they more readily affect a person's behavior. Intellectual conversion can often be discerned through questions, but children may have difficulty describing feelings. The observations of parents, sponsors and team members play an important role in discerning conversion. Even when a child or parent may not be able to articulate conversion, the observations of others may provide evidence that conversion has taken place.

The Intellectual Dimension

Stephen Owens was an intelligent, polite, friendly, likable third-grade student at St. Anthony School. He knew a lot of Scripture verses. He could name the seven sacraments and recite many Catholic facts. He attended school liturgies and knew all the parts of the Mass. Everyone thought the process of initiation would be short and simple for Stephen. There didn't appear to be any areas of his life where he needed conversion.

Therefore, even Stephen was surprised by how much his relationship with God and the community changed throughout the course of the catechumenate. Stephen knew a lot of facts and stories about God, Jesus and the Church, but the catechumenal process of breaking open the word helped Stephen take those stories to heart. Stephen came to know God, the Scriptures and the Church in a new way.

Knowing, seeing, hearing or understanding

in a new way is conversion. Intellectual conversion means moving from knowing about something to understanding its meaning. In Stephen's case, his whole life did not drastically change, but his knowledge of God and Church changed to a relationship with God and Church. His knowledge of Scripture verses changed into knowledge of stories that described our loving God, Jesus the Christ and the community of Jesus' disciples. Stephen was not bored by a "review" of Scripture and doctrine that he already knew. On the contrary, he was intrigued by the process of delving into the Scriptures Sunday after Sunday. He asked lots of questions and was enthusiastic about the gatherings.

Intellectual conversion also happens in children who are not necessarily knowledgeable about Scripture and doctrine. John and Maggie came to the initiation process well informed of the "fact" that God loved them. Their mother was a returning Catholic and their stepfather was also a candidate for initiation. Their parents had taught them about God's love, but both children talked about God's love in a matter-of-fact, detached, unemotional way. The "fact" of God's love had little meaning for them. They had not made the connection that their parents' love was a reflection of God's love.

During the course of the catechumenate, a great deal of growth occurred in their family. A marriage annulment was a long, difficult process for their mother and stepfather, but it helped resolve some family issues. Maggie went through a phase where she didn't participate in the initiation process or in church. She eventually received help from a counselor. John remained stoic at first, but later began to actively add to the discussions. At the time of the final discernment, each one spoke of their certainty of God's love. Each, in different ways, talked about God's love being evident in the love of their family. Maggie

particularly mentioned her grandmother being a sign of God's love for her. John spoke of feeling God's love in the parish.

Thus, Maggie and John moved from intellectual knowledge of God's love to an experience of God's love that they could name and describe.

In addition, intellectual conversion also includes "an appropriate acquaintance with dogmas and precepts" (#75.1). In other words, part of the conversion process for children includes becoming familiar with the doctrine and dogmas of the community. Becoming a part of any family, one assimilates the teaching and tradition of the family. However, the Rite is careful to say an "appropriate acquaintance with dogmas and precepts." Earlier in #75.1, a "suitable catechesis" is described as being provided for the children. These descriptions highlight the nature of the teaching the catechumens are to receive. Child catechumens and candidates are not asked to learn a complete catechism. Rather, they are expected to move from relatively little knowledge and understanding of Church teaching to a basic understanding of the meaning of important "dogmas and precepts." Those important dogmas and precepts are unfolded throughout the course of the liturgical year.

In general, intellectual conversion has to do with understanding the meaning of what the Church believes. The child does not need to know all Church doctrine. The religious education that follows initiation will help in the teaching of doctrine. Since many children come to the catechumenate with little background in the Church, even an acquaintance with doctrine is a great deal for them to digest. Nonetheless, when catechized correctly, a familiarity with the teachings of the community is part of the intellectual conversion of the child.

Intellectual conversion also includes the child's having acquired a "profound sense of the mystery of salvation" (#75.1). Learning doctrine, dogma and precepts has little value if it is not also accompanied by a sense of the mystery of salvation. Understanding to some extent what it means to be saved by the power of God through Jesus Christ in the Holy Spirit is a large part of the process of conversion. Believing in the mystery of salvation is not solely confined to intellectual conversion. The mystery of salvation envelops the whole person.

The Moral Dimension

From the time they walked into the parish office, Maggie and John's dislike for one another was evident. They sat far apart and did not look at one another. Although they spoke to the initiation director and to their parents, they rarely spoke to one another. In the early precatechumenate sessions, their behavior toward one another remained the same. There were occasional verbal jabs and glares exchanged between them. Their mother was bothered by their dislike or intolerance of each other, but she attributed the behavior to "just being teenagers."

As they moved into the catechumenate period, their attitude and actions toward one another began to warm. They listened more respectfully to one another when one of them was making a comment. The jabs and glares diminished, then disappeared. As the catechumenate progressed, they even laughed and joked with one another.

Their mother and stepfather noticed the change. Their parents explained their "new" relationship as partly the result of maturation, but mostly the result of hearing the gospel week after week. Their stepfather said, "I think they started to really listen to the words of Jesus and take them to heart."

Moral conversion is evidenced by a change in a child's actions and attitudes. It involves the child's personal response to the gospel.

When a child truly hears and takes to heart the Good News, his or her behavior will be affected. The behavioral change may be subtle, like being more helpful or less argumentative at home. Or, the change may be more noticeable, as in the case of Maggie and John. Sometimes, parents notice a change in a child that goes unnoticed by the child. When Maggie and John discussed how the initiation process had affected their lives, they did not mention the change in their behavior toward one another. Once it was pointed out, however, they recognized that conversion was taking place in their relationship.

The Church looks for the catechumens "to bear witness to the faith...to practice love of neighbor, even at the cost of self-renunciation" (#75.2). "To bear witness to the faith" means that the child's actions testify to her or his developing faith. Maggie and John's improved relationship was a testimony to the power of God's word in their lives. Their actions bore witness to their faith in Jesus Christ and his message. Not only did their parents notice the change, but the catechumenal group felt the change. The group was much more at ease without the tension between Maggie and John. Undoubtedly, friends and neighbors would also notice the change. John and Maggie had come to practice "love of neighbor" right in their own home.

Moral conversion can be manifested by a change in attitude as well as action. A child's attitude toward race, gender, poverty, sexuality, war and peace, AIDS/HIV, abortion, euthanasia and other issues may be affected by the initiation process.

For about five months during the breaking open the word sessions at Our Lady of Good Counsel Parish, questions and comments about racism regularly entered the discussion. There had been two incidents of blatant racism in the public school system that year. Although I cannot specifically verify that the attitudes of the catechumens and candidates changed, I can verify that all the catechumens, candidates, parents and sponsors reconsidered their attitudes about race. A step on the path to moral conversion was taken.

In general, moral conversion is manifested through the child's lived response. The child responds to the gospel message by acting differently, as in the case of Maggie and John, or the child responds with a change in attitude toward family, school, other people or issues.

The Social Dimension

Anthony was passive, timid and withdrawn when he first started the initiation process. He and his father came to the sessions together and for the first few weeks, Anthony spoke to and interacted with others very little. By the following year, Anthony became a leader in the youth group, and he was always one of the first to share in a discussion in the catechumenal group. He eagerly volunteered for service with the youth group, working at youth group dances and helping to cook the Thanksgiving meal at the parish's residence for senior citizens.

Anthony experienced social conversion in that he moved from feeling as though he were a stranger in the Christian community to feeling that he belonged. He moved from a feeling of being outside to a feeling of being inside.

Anthony's father was an inactive Catholic. He, too, saw himself as outside the Church. Through the initiation process, Anthony and his father came to see themselves as part of the larger Christian community. As members of the community, they also saw themselves as responsible for the mission of the community. As Anthony worked with the youth group, his father also became involved in the group's activities. He often chaperoned or volunteered to drive to events.

Social conversion for a child also includes the broader community beyond the Church.

The child comes to understand that as a sister or brother of Jesus, she or he is united with all people through the power of the Spirit. Any change from seeing oneself as an individual to seeing oneself as united with the larger community is social conversion.

During breaking open the word one Sunday morning, Kimberly commented on "praying or doing something" for the children in Bosnia. She felt not only connected, but responsible, for the children in Bosnia. She evidenced a sign of social and moral conversion.

Summary

Conversion in a child is as unique and individual as each child. One child may experience one dimension of conversion and another child may experience all four dimensions of conversion. Other children may experience other dimensions or types of conversion that were not discussed here, for example, religious, attitudinal, behavioral or theistic conversion. Further, a child may experience a type of conversion that cannot be named. What is most important is that the process of initiation does make a difference in the life of the child and her or his family.

Discerning Conversion

Discerning conversion in a child is a distinct honor and a serious responsibility. It is an honor in that one is in a place to observe, hear and witness God actively working in the life of a child. It is also an honor to watch the child discover that the Spirit is indeed at work in his or her life.

Moreover, those who help with the discernment process have been entrusted by the Church with a serious responsibility. The Rite states that before catechumens are admitted to the Rite of Election, a "judgment" is to be made regarding their readiness:

Before the rite of election the bishop, priests, deacons, catechists, godparents, and the entire community, in accord with their respective responsibilities, and in their own way, should, after considering the matter carefully, arrive at a judgment about the catechumens' state of formation and progress (#121).

For children, the Rite's list of those who determine readiness would also include parents. In addition to "conversion in mind and action," the children are expected to have an "acquaintance with Christian teaching as well as a spirit of faith and charity" (#121). These are the signs that indicate the child is ready to celebrate the Rite of Election and, thereafter, the sacraments of initiation.

There are several ways to discern conversion in a child. One way is to gather the godparents, sponsors, family and child for a "discernment interview." The interview takes place at the child's home, at the parish office or wherever the child is most comfortable. The gathering is an informal time for family and sponsors to give testimony about the various dimensions of conversion they have seen in the child. Likewise, the child may testify on her or his own behalf. Often, a young child will talk more about what he or she has "learned" instead of how the process has affected her or his life. In this case, the parents, godparents and sponsors talk about the life changes they have observed. Another option is to have only the child and immediate family at the interview. Sponsors and godparents would be consulted separately.

The initiation team determines who conducts the interview. The interviewer may be the initiation coordinator, the pastor, or a qualified spiritual director who has been involved with the family throughout the process. The discussion has a broad point of departure and then narrows to a particular dimension of conversion if there seems to be

one. The interview is conducted in a prayerful, reflective, peaceful atmosphere.

After warmly greeting the family and making sure all are comfortable, the interviewer begins with an opening prayer and then continues in this or a similar way:

> We're here today to talk about Tonya's readiness to take the next step on the path toward the celebration of the sacraments. Tonya feels that she is ready to move ahead and celebrate the Rite of Election. Tonya, would you talk about why you want to be baptized and received into the Church?
>
> Can you, her family and friends, talk about why you feel Tonya is ready for the Rite of Election? Specifically, can you tell me how you have seen any changes in her life?

After the family and sponsors speak, the interviewer should ask a question that follows up on what has been said. Depending on the responses given, this question could focus on the area of conversion that coincides with the testimony. Also, the questions need to be adapted to the age and maturity of the child. Some possible questions or discussion starters are given below. Or, the questions may be adapted and asked of parents regarding their children. The interviewer considers whether the child's or parent's response shows growth from when they started the process.

Affective Conversion

- Describe for me (us) your feelings about God.
- Describe for me (us) your feelings about belonging to the Church.
- Has being involved in this initiation process changed your feelings about family, friends or classmates? How so?

Intellectual Conversion

■ How would you describe God? Jesus? The Holy Spirit?

■ Tell me about one of your favorite Scripture stories. What does it mean?

■ Tell me some things you like or don't like about the Church? Why?

Moral Conversion

■ Do you feel that you act any differently toward your family or friends since you have been involved in the Church? How so?

■ What are some ways that you have become more like Jesus?

Social Conversion

■ What makes you feel at home in this parish community?

■ How does becoming a Christian affect your relationship with other people?

■ What new responsibilities will you have when you become a Christian?

These questions are examples of discussion starters meant to provide a glimpse into the child's journey of conversion. The child's responses, the family's and sponsor's responses and their observations of the child, and the initiation team's observations, combine to help determine if the child has experienced conversion and is ready for initiation.

Another way to discern readiness for the Rite of Election is for the parish to host a "formal day of discernment."[15] At St. Rose of Lima Parish in Gaithersburg, Maryland, sponsors meet with the catechumens and candidates to do preliminary discernment. Then, closer to the time of election, a formal day of discernment is hosted in which catechumens, candidates, sponsors, team members, family, companions and other parishioners meet for a day of discernment.

The entire group gathers for a day of prayer and reflection. The pastor asks the sponsors to give testimony regarding "the areas of Christian formation described in the Rite (#75)."[16] Others are also invited to testify about the readiness of the person. The candidates and catechumens are encouraged to speak for themselves. This type of day is a good example of an intergenerational gathering where children and adults are together for a day.

Whether discernment is done through an interview process or through a parish day of discernment, the importance and seriousness of the task is not to be overlooked. Some initiation teams presume that because a child has participated in an initiation process, she or he is ready for election and, subsequently, for initiation. The Rite is clear that readiness for initiation includes conversion. Discerning conversion in a child requires family input, testimony from catechists, sponsors and godparents (#278), respectful observation of the child, prayer and conversation with the catechumen or candidate.

The Rite of Election

When the catechumens have completed the period of the catechumenate and have exhibited conversion, they take the second step in the journey of initiation: the celebration of the Rite of Election in which the Church makes its "election," that is, its choice, to admit those catechumens who will celebrate the sacraments of initiation (#119). In other words, the celebration of the Rite of Election presumes the child will celebrate the sacraments of initiation unless there is some serious impediment.

In the first section of Part II of the Rite of Christian Initiation of Adults, the Rite of Election, or Enrollment of Names (#277-290), is optional for children. The Rite does not say why election is optional, but it does say that the rite "may be celebrated with children of catechetical age, especially those whose catechumenate has extended over a long period of time" (#277). The authors of the Rite give no reason why children should not celebrate the Rite of Election.

It seems to me that if the rite is beneficial for those who have had a long period of formation, it is also beneficial for those who have had a shorter period of formation. Being "elected" by God through the voice of the Church makes children feel special and chosen. For indeed they are.

The Rite of Election is the second step of the initiation process and begins the period of final preparation for the sacraments of initiation, during which the children will be encouraged to follow Christ with greater generosity (#277). Omitting the Rite of Election means that the "second step" becomes the Scrutinies (#291). That is, since there is no Rite of Election, the Scrutinies mark the beginning of the final period of preparation. This is problematic because the Scrutinies are penitential rites. The purpose of the Scrutinies is not election, nor is their purpose transition to the period of purification and enlightenment. Omitting the Rite of Election means the children do not have the transitory step from the second period to the third period. And they are denied the formative experience of being ritually chosen as members of God's elect.

Part II says that when the Rite of Election is celebrated with child and adult catechumens, "the rite for adults (#129-137) should be used, with appropriate adaptation of the texts to be made by the celebrant" (#279). Typically, the Rite of Election is celebrated at the cathedral with children and adults. There might be pastoral reasons, however, for the Rite of Election to be celebrated in the parish with only children. For example, there may be only

child catechumens in the parish, or it may not be possible to go to the cathedral for the celebration with the bishop and other catechumens. When the Rite of Election is at the cathedral, the Rite of Sending the Catechumens for Election is celebrated in the parish with children and adults. There is no rite of sending given only for children in Part II.

Celebrating the Rite of Election With Children

The Rite of Election, or Enrollment of Names, given for children in Part II (#281-290) is written in such a way that presumes that only children are being presented for election. Let's take a look at that rite.

Liturgy of the Word

The rite is to be celebrated "within Mass." This is a change from the Rite of Acceptance with children, which was "not normally combined with the celebration of the eucharist" (#261). The rite is also to be celebrated on the First Sunday of Lent (#280). This presumably means celebrated with the Sunday assembly. Therefore, a relatively large number of people would be present. This is also a change from #257, which says the Rite of Acceptance is to be celebrated with a small, active representation of the parish. If the celebration of the Rite of Election is at the cathedral with the bishop, the assembly would most likely be rather large, and many diocesan celebrations do not include the Eucharist.

Homily

In the first rubric of the rite, #281 suggests that a catechist or other adult give the homily, if the celebrant finds it difficult "to adapt himself to the mentality of the children." Having a catechist or another qualified adult give a homily for children is not without precedent. The *Directory for Masses with Children*, #24, also states that an adult may speak after the gospel. Because the other rites in Part II do not offer this option, it may have been given with the bishop in mind, since the bishop is the presiding celebrant for the Rite of Election.

Presentation of the Children

When the children are presented, they come forward with their parents and godparents. The godparents chosen by the child may be different from the parish sponsor who stood with them at the Rite of Acceptance (#10, 11). Although the child's godparents accompany the child and parents at election, the parish sponsors may still be present. If the child and parents choose godparents other than the parish sponsors, the sponsors still continue in their role as parish sponsors. The sponsors' presence at the rite may be an appropriate adaptation. Likewise, the sponsors and the godparents could both be present at the upcoming Scrutinies.

Affirmation by the Parents, Godparents [and the Assembly]

The celebrant addresses a series of questions to the parents, godparents and the assembly. The questions are intended to be a "recommendation" of the children (#283). This can be done for a group of children if there are a great many. A more personal way to give testimony about the children, however, is for a parent or godparent to testify on behalf of each child.

The "recommendation" questions given in #283 are helpful for another reason: They give the community an idea of what has happened during the time of catechumenal formation. For example, the children are asked if they "listened well to the word of God," "tried to live as faithful followers" and participated in the "community's life of prayer and service." This tells the community that this is what the children did during the catechumenate. They listened to God's word, they learned to live as disciples and they learned prayer and service.

Invitation and Enrollment of Names

The children are asked to state their intention to become full members of the Church. Then they are asked to offer their names for enrollment. The Rite (#284) offers several ways in which the children can offer their names for enrollment. If the rite is at the cathedral, the presentation of a list may be necessary. If a list is presented at the cathedral, then the children would sign the Book of the Elect at the parish Rite of Sending. Whatever the case, I recommend that the children sign the book themselves at some point. Inscribing their names in the book emphasizes that the children are making a serious commitment. It is also a strong statement about commitment for the assembly when they see the young people carefully and deliberately enter their names among the elect.

Act of Admission or Election

The children are accepted as the elect. The parents and godparents receive the children into their care by placing a hand on their shoulder or by some other gesture.

[Recognition of Godparents]

The recognition of godparents is optional. It is a prayer that speaks of the new relationship between parents and godparents. The Church prays that they will support one another. Understandably, this prayer is not necessary for adults and thus is not given as an option in Part I.

Intercession for the Elect, Prayer Over the Elect, Dismissal of the Elect

The rite concludes in the same way as the adult rite does. The Church prays for the elect and then the celebrant dismisses them prior to the Liturgy of the Eucharist.

Liturgy of the Eucharist

The children are dismissed from the rite and go with their catechist for breaking open the word. After Mass, an unpacking of the rite takes place with their parents, godparents and sponsors. If there is no Liturgy of the Eucharist, as often is the case if the celebration is at the cathedral with the bishop, the unpacking of the rite could occur at a later time.

Finally, as with adults, if there are children who are catechumens for election and baptized candidates who are preparing to receive Confirmation and Eucharist and make a profession of faith, a combined rite for catechumens and candidates may be used. While candidates do not celebrate the Rite of Election, they do celebrate a Call to Continuing Conversion. The combined rite for catechumens and candidates is found in Appendix I of the *Rite*. Since combined rites are not given for children, the combined rite for adults is used and adapted as needed.

Preparing for the Rite of Election

In preparing the catechumens for the Rite of Election and candidates for the Call to Continuing Conversion, a process of preparation similar to the preparation for the Rite of Acceptance is used. Discernment is an important part of preparation for the rite. Formal discernment is necessary. Then, a preparation session serves as a more immediate preparation for the rite.

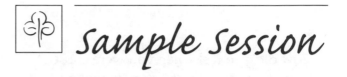

Sample Session

A Preparation Session for the Rite of Election

Once again, the preparation session is part of the larger process of liturgical catechesis. The preparation session helps the child and family fully enter into the liturgical experience. For the Rite of Election, the preparation session focuses on the symbol of the book and of election. The session may take place on a Sunday after the breaking open of the word.

- Gathering and Introduction
- My Story and God's Story
- Reflection on Signing
- Connecting With the Rite
- Closing Ritual

Gathering and Introduction

This session may be the first time that godparents are part of the group. New folks need a special welcome and introduction. Some explanation of the Rite of Election is needed.

My Story and God's Story

In this movement, a discussion or activity helps the families focus on the idea of being chosen or elected. The purpose is to connect personal or family experience of being chosen with the stories of God's "choosing" or calling people.

In family groups or another type of intergenerational grouping, ask each person to name a time when they were chosen (for example, chosen to be on a sporting team, chosen by a teacher to be leader or helper, chosen by a parent or grandparent to do a job or receive an award, elected to a public office).

When the group has finished, ask them to discuss the following:

■ How did you feel when you were chosen?
■ How did you feel just before you were chosen, while you were waiting to be chosen?
■ Who chose you?
■ Why were you chosen?

Next, ask the members of each group to name a person from Scripture, history or their own lives whom God chose (for example, Moses, Abraham and Sarah, Queen Esther, Peter, James, John, Mary, Martha, Dr. Martin Luther King, Jr., someone in their family, the pastor). Then ask them to identify how the person's life was changed by God's call.

After those in the small groups have shared their answers among themselves, they can share with the large group.

Reflection on Signing

A primary symbolic action of the Rite of Election is the signing of one's name in the Book of the Elect. A discussion, activity or meditation helps the children reflect on signing their names in the Book of the Elect.

Ask two or three adults to tell the group about an official document they have signed. What did their signature mean?

Then, move into small intergenerational groups and ask each person to think of time when they have signed their name. Discuss: What does signing your name mean?

Connecting With the Rite

Talk with the children about the Rite of Election in general terms. There is no need to describe the rite fully. Discuss how God chooses the children and how they accept the call. Also, talk to the children and the adults about the role of the bishop and why the celebration is at the cathedral.

(Note: There are various opinions about how much to "explain" before a rite. The rite needs to speak for itself and then be unpacked after the experience. Telling the children "what the rite means" predisposes them to experience it in a certain way. Nonetheless, I find it helpful to talk briefly about what is being celebrated, about the bishop and about the cathedral.)

Give the children reflection questions to talk about with their parents, godparents and sponsors. Other children and adults in the group may also respond to the questions. The responses the catechumens give may be incorporated into the testimony the godparents give during the Rite of Election. If there is not adequate time during the session for the discussion, the children may meet with the godparents or sponsors at another time.

Here are some sample questions, adapted from questions found in the rite (#283):

■ Why do you want to become a full member of this community?
■ How does listening to God's word help you?
■ How have you tried to be a follower of Jesus?
■ How would you describe the way you pray?

Closing Ritual

Ask the small groups to come together for the closing ritual. Invite the catechumens and candidates to move to the center of the room. Use one of the blessings for catechumens (#95-97).

Catechist: Please extend your hands over the catechumens and candidates.

Let us pray.

> Lord God,
> you desire that all children be saved
> and come into your loving arms.
> Strengthen the faith of these children who
>   are preparing for Baptism, Confirmation
>   and Eucharist; bring them into your
>   Church,

there to receive the gift of eternal life.
We ask this through Christ our Lord.
Amen.
(#97.G, adapted.)

Rehearsing for the Rite of Election

Briefly walking through key parts of the rite
with parents and godparents is sufficient
preparation. Children will feel comfortable and
confident knowing their parents and/or
godparents stand with them.

Reflection Session After the Rite of Election

Once again, the unpacking session after the
Rite of Election is the same process as that
used after the Rite of Acceptance. The children
reflect upon what they experienced in the rite
and what that experience meant to them (see
Chapter Three, pages 51-54).

Catechesis and the Rite of Election

The Rite of Election brings to culmination the
period of the catechumenate and points ahead
to what will come in the period of purification
and enlightenment. Remember, a major rite
gives insight into what the "content" for
catechesis and formation is for the periods that
both precede and succeed it.

Studying the Rite of Election shows the
initiation team what the Church expects of its
catechumens before they celebrate the Rite of
Election. First, the Rite refers to the children's
"dispositions" and "desire for" the sacraments
of initiation (#278, #283). In order for children
to have such a desire and be disposed to the

sacraments, they necessarily would have some
acquaintance with the sacraments of initiation.
In other words, reflection on the sacramental
symbols would be part of their formation.

Second, the Rite asks parents and
godparents if the children have listened well to
the word of God (#283). The question points to
the priority God's word has in the formation of
the children. The question is also reminiscent
of #75.1, which says that catechesis is to be
based on the word. Children gathering with
the Sunday assembly each week to hear the
word proclaimed, followed by the breaking
open of the word helps ensure that the
children have every opportunity to listen well
to the word of God.

Further, the Rite also asks about the
children being "faithful followers" who
participate in the "community's life of prayer
and service." Once again, #75 is recalled. The
children's catechumenal formation includes
community (#75.2), prayer (#75.2) and
apostolic service (#75.4). In addition to
catechesis, the Church expects the children to
have been formed by the community's life of
prayer and service.

Pointing Ahead

In regard to pointing ahead to the upcoming
period of purification and enlightenment, the
intercessions for the children (#287) provide
insight. The Church prays that the Lenten
season, their final period of preparation, will
be a time of "genuine Christian renewal." The
prayers also ask that the children will grow in
their love of God, neighbor and the Church
and that they will be "freed from selfishness."
In general, the prayers indicate the time ahead
will be a prayerful time of growth. Indeed,
prayer and reflection are the centerpieces for
the Lenten season, the usual time for the
period of purification and enlightenment.

Summary

The catechumenate is an extensive period filled with reflections on Scripture, liturgical catechesis, rites, rituals, community involvement, prayer, service, family time and fun time for children. The period of the catechumenate may last months or years. It is a time for child catechumens and candidates to deepen their relationship with the living God. It is a time for them to deepen their understanding of God's word and the Church doctrines that flow from that word. It is a time for them to bond with the Christian community and learn the community's ways of prayer and service. The catechumenate is a time for the children to grow in their commitment to family and those outside of family. Lastly, the period of the catechumenate is a time of faith development not only for the children but also for their entire family as well.

REFERENCES

[1] Paragraph 75 refers to the formation of catechumens, but adaptation allows for baptized candidates to be included as well.

[2] Walter M. Abbott, S.J., ed., "Constitution on the Sacred Liturgy," *The Documents of Vatican II* (Chicago: Follett Publishing Co., 1966), paragraph 10, p. 142.

[3] Ibid., paragraph 102, p. 168. (Emphasis added)

[4] Pope Paul VI, Apostolic Constitution, Promulgation of the Roman Missal, 3 April 1969.

[5] I first learned a method for preparing breaking open the word with adults at a Beginnings and Beyond Institute presented by the North American Forum on the Catechumenate. I have adapted the method for use with breaking open the word with children.

[6] Linda Gaupin, C.D.P., has greatly influenced my thinking on sacramental catechesis. The method presented here is adapted from a presentation given by Linda Gaupin to catechetical leaders in the Archdiocese of Detroit. She called the process of using a liturgical symbol to lead persons to the mystery of the sacraments, "Cracking Open the Symbols." I have adapted what I learned from her for use with child catechumens, candidates and their families.

[7] Gaupin.

[8] Kevin Bourassa, who is a team liturgist with the North American Forum on the Catechumenate and Director of Music and Liturgy, St. Mary Cathedral Parish Community, Diocese of Saginaw, first encouraged me to intone prayers with children.

[9] Ernest Evans, ed., trans., *Tertullian's Homily on Baptism* (Cambridge: University Printing House, 1964), p. 39.

[10] Ibid.

[11] Burton Scott Easton, ed., trans., *The Apostolic Tradition of Hippolytus* (New York: Cambridge University Press, 1962), p. 45.

[12] "Two Historical Precedents" is from an article first published in "What Should We Ask of Child Catechumens?," *Catechumenate: A Journal of Christian Initiation*, September 1991, p. 14.

[13] Regis Duffy, *On Becoming a Catholic: The Challenge of Christian Initiation* (San Francisco: Harper and Row, 1984), p. vii. Duffy mentions these four dimensions of catechumenal formation in the introduction to his book.

[14] Beginnings and Beyond Institute: Participant Packet. (Falls Church, Va.: The North American Forum on the Catechumenate, 1995), p. 19.

[15] Robert D. Duggan, "Discernment of Readiness: Where is Solomon When We Need Him?", *Catechumenate: A Journal of Christian Initiation*, January 1995, pp. 7-9. Duggan describes a discernment process at St. Rose of Lima Parish.

[16] Ibid., p. 8.

5

The Period of Purification and Enlightenment

The preparation session for the First Scrutiny went exceptionally well. The children recognized the evil that surrounded them. They spoke of forces that scared them. They named weaknesses they saw in themselves. Marc fully and sincerely participated in the reflection.

Two days later, Marc's mother called. Marc was in serious trouble. His mother had removed all his privileges, and he was restricted for a month. The teacher and principal at school were also involved. The discernment process regarding Marc had been completed, and everyone had felt that he was more than ready for initiation. Now his parents, the initiation director, the pastor and Marc himself wondered if his conversion was really complete.

During the period of purification and enlightenment, the Scrutinies "should complete the conversion of the elect" (#141). When Marc got into trouble, his mother's immediate reaction was that Marc must not be ready for initiation. Marc's mother thought the conversion that Marc and his parents had previously identified must have been insincere. Not only had Marc and his friend harassed classmates, but Marc lied about it afterward. Could such a person be ready for initiation in just five weeks?

After several lengthy discussions with the initiation director and the pastor, Marc and his family decided to wait until after the Scrutinies to make the final decision about whether or not Marc should be baptized. Marc expressed heartfelt remorse. I spoke with Marc and his parents about the purpose of the Scrutinies, and all agreed that celebrating the Scrutinies was the right step for Marc. For the Scrutinies "are meant to uncover, then heal all that is weak, defective, or sinful in the hearts of the elect; to bring out, then strengthen all that is upright, strong and good" (#141). Marc felt he had a weakness for peer pressure and that his actions had been sinful. He still wanted to be baptized, and he felt that he was ready for initiation, but he had really "messed up."

After celebrating the three Scrutinies, Marc and his parents talked again with the director and pastor about the meaning of conversion. Marc felt that the Scrutinies had helped him see that God could help him. He said the Scrutinies "made me feel stronger."

In the end, everyone agreed that one step backward on the journey was a part of life for all people. Marc celebrated the sacraments of initiation at the Easter Vigil. And, Marc reports, he has not been in serious trouble since.

Spiritual Recollection

The period of purification and enlightenment is a time of "spiritual recollection" (#138) for children who are the "elect" and for those who are candidates for full communion with the Catholic Church. Because nothing is said regarding children about this particular period in the first section of Part II except for the paragraphs on the Scrutinies (#291-303), Part I is used as the guide for this period.

The Rite is explicit about the purpose of the period (#138, 139): to purify and enlighten the elect and candidates in order to prepare them fully for the celebration of the sacraments of initiation at the Easter Vigil. The third period is a time of "intense spiritual preparation," as the elect, candidates and the faithful prepare to celebrate the paschal mystery.

Furthermore, the period of purification and enlightenment is a time for "liturgical catechesis" rather than "catechetical instruction" (#138, 139). The celebration of the Scrutinies and the Presentations of the Creed and the Lord's Prayer are primary means by which the elect and candidates are purified and enlightened. Liturgical catechesis in this period includes the preparation for the Scrutinies and Presentations, the celebrations themselves, and the reflection after each celebration.

As part of their Lenten liturgical catechesis, the elect and candidates continue to celebrate the Liturgy of the Word with the Sunday assembly and break open the word afterward. Rather than a catechetical session following the breaking open the word, there would be the reflection on the Scrutiny on the third, fourth and fifth Sundays of Lent. The Presentations are also celebrated during Lent. The Scrutinies and Presentations are the foundation of the forty-day Lenten "retreat" for the elect.

Scrutinies and Children

The retreat-like nature of the Lenten season is built largely upon the Scrutinies, which help the children examine their lives and see where they may need to reform and repent. The Scrutinies free the children from the forces of evil that keep them in darkness.

Evil in the Life of a Child

There is no question that children experience sin and evil in their lives and thus benefit from the celebration of the Scrutinies. Some catechists and pastoral ministers, however, feel there is little need for the Scrutinies for children. Likewise, the Rite provides only one "Penitential Rite (Scrutiny)" for children that is much different and milder than the adult rite. The Rite suggests that a second be celebrated if convenient (#294). However, the reality of evil is as strongly present in the life of a child as it is in the life of an adult. And evil can be even more devastating and life-threatening for children. Therefore, I recommend that all three Scrutinies be celebrated to help "deliver the elect from the power of Satan" (#141) and give the children strength to persevere in their journey.

According to Dick Westly, evil is that which frustrates a vital human need, desire or interest.[1] In other words, evil is a force, or power, that works against life. There are forces or powers constantly working against the needs of children. The basic human needs of many children are frustrated, or unfulfilled, every day. One in four children in the United States lives in poverty. They do not have decent food or housing. Many parents cannot provide adequate health care for their children because they are uninsured and medical costs are prohibitive. Shortly before Easter one year, I was casually talking with a mother and asked how her youngest child was. She expressed concern over a nagging cough the child had. I quickly and matter-of-factly said, "What does the doctor say?" She replied, "I don't know, I can't afford to take him." I was abruptly taken aback. There is a systemic evil present in a society that does not take proper care of its children.

Evil is present not only in society at large, but within children's homes. Children need to have a secure, stable family and home life. An inordinate number of children live in abusive homes where violence is a regular occurrence. Children witness violence to others in their homes, and they themselves are victims of physical, emotional and sexual abuse. Even if there is not violence in the home, a child's need for security and stability is nonetheless frustrated when divorce, separation, loss or death visits the home.[2] In one group of catechumens and candidates with which I worked, every one of the seven children had recently experienced the death or serious illness of someone significant in their lives.

Not only does evil frustrate the basic human needs of children, evil also frustrates the desires of children. Children have a natural desire to laugh, to play, to act silly, to run, to "mess around" and simply "be a kid." Many children have little opportunity to engage in carefree, unhurried, uninterrupted play. Some children are burdened by the necessary responsibilities of taking care of younger siblings. Some children live in an environment where abuse or neglect keeps them from enjoying the simple pleasures of childhood because they fear for their own safety. Some children do not get a chance to express their desires because their parent(s) are too busy with their own responsibilities and problems.

I was once sitting in a Burger King (with a children's play area), and I overheard a mother hurriedly saying to her three-year-old daughter, "Hurry up and eat, so you can play.

We have to go." The little girl was hurrying to eat, just to have some time to play. This is a mild example of the way many children get rushed from one point to the next. Some are rushed from the time they wake and go to before-school care, until the time they are picked up from school and go to soccer, piano, scouts or dance and then home in time for homework and bed. When natural desires and interests are squelched, a child has encountered evil.

In addition to being victims of evil, children may also be capable of committing serious sin. Recently in Anderson, Indiana, a fourteen-year-old boy was convicted of murdering an eight-year-old girl. A priest who works with abused children told me that some of the violent offenders he counsels are seven years old and their victims are five years old. Some high schools have installed metal detectors because so many students carry knives and guns to school. Other examples of children being capable of sin are less physically violent, but still damaging. Sixth-grade girls taunted Mindy because of the color of her skin. Brent refuses to ride the bus to school because the other children are so mean to him. Children have the capacity to be cruel and abusive to other children and to adults as well.

Be they victims or perpetrators of evil, children want to be freed from the evil that surrounds and entraps them. The evil that surrounds a child may be felt most intensely in the home, where the child is caught in a cycle of poverty or abuse that has continued from generation to generation. Or, the evil may manifest itself in the local community, where lonely, searching, troubled young people turn to gangs. Or, the evil may be most evident for the child at school, where ridicule and hate cause daily pain.

Children can identify the forces of society that lead to evil. They recognize racism, alcoholism, drug dependency, poverty and violence as evils in society. Even though they may not be able to name the deeper societal ills that lead to the manifestation of evil, children know that evil exists in their world. On the other hand, sometimes all the child knows is that there is anger and fighting at home, and she or he wants it to stop. Whether it is a huge societal evil such as racism or an individual evil such as impatience and intolerance, children long to be free from the problems that darken their world.

The Penitential Rite (Scrutiny) for Children (#295-302)

The Scrutinies are celebrated to strengthen the elect and free them from darkness and sin. The Rite provides one Penitential Rite (Scrutiny) for children in the first section of Part II. Three Scrutinies for adults are given in Part I. Several major differences are evident between the Scrutinies for adults and the Penitential Rite (Scrutiny) for children. Both the name and the nature of the children's rite is different from the adult rite.

The nature of the Scrutinies is described in the Rite as one of self-searching, repentance, healing and strengthening. The Scrutinies help the elect examine their lives and strengthen their resolve to live as faithful followers of Christ. The Scrutinies "complete the conversion" of the elect and ready them for the celebration of Baptism, Confirmation and Eucharist.

A penitential rite has a purpose similar to a Scrutiny, but it is intended for those who are already baptized. While the adult rite in Part I is a Scrutiny, the children's rite in Part II is a "Penitential Rite (Scrutiny)." Note that the word *scrutiny* is in parentheses after the words *penitential rite*. The Rite of Christian Initiation of Adults is careful to differentiate between the Scrutinies and the Penitential Rite because

"baptized companions from the catechetical group participate in the celebration of these penitential rites" (#293). If the rite is a penitential rite, then baptized companions can participate. If the rite is a Scrutiny, only the unbaptized elect would participate. The name of the rite indicates it is both a Scrutiny and a penitential rite since both the elect and the baptized participate.

Later in Part II, the fifth section, "Preparation of Uncatechized Adults for Confirmation and Eucharist, Optional Rites for Baptized but Uncatechized Adults" (#463), urges that the Scrutinies for the elect and the Penitential Rite for those preparing for Confirmation and Eucharist be kept "separate and distinct." There seems to be a discrepancy here.

Another significant issue to consider is that the Rite says that the Penitential Rite is "a proper occasion for baptized children of the catechetical group to celebrate the sacrament of penance for the first time" (#293). This is a rather awkward addition to the Penitential Rite, for now the elect and their baptized companions celebrate the Penitential Rite and then the baptized children celebrate the sacrament of penance. No mention is made of children who are candidates for full communion with the Catholic Church. Since other baptized children are celebrating the rite, the baptized candidates could presumably participate and may receive the sacrament of penance.

My personal participation in a children's Penitential Rite (Scrutiny) combined with the sacrament of penance leads me to believe the combination is problematic. The celebration was a disaster! Granted, there could have been other reasons why the celebration was poor, but trying to unite the liturgy of penance with the Penitential Rite (Scrutiny) was contrived and ineffective. The celebrant seemed to be talking to two different groups of people in the assembly. The elect, the candidates for full communion and the candidates for penance were unclear as to who was who and what was what. Although that was only one celebration and could certainly be improved upon, a Penitential Rite (Scrutiny) without the sacrament of penance added on would have been better for the elect, the candidates and the entire assembly.

A rationale for the liturgy of penance being added to the Penitential Rite (Scrutiny) is not given in the Rite. Many liturgists speculate that the liturgy of penance was added as a way of bolstering the reception of the sacrament. Given that a Scrutiny for children has a penitential tone, perhaps it seemed like a chance to have baptized children go to confession. Considering that the Rite of Christian Initiation of Adults was being written at approximately the same time as the debate over the reception of penance and its praxis were in high gear, this speculation seems tenable.

Other questions surround the rite. The entire structure of the rite for children is different from that for adults. The adult rite is to take place during Mass on the Third, Fourth and Fifth Sundays of Lent (#146). The children's rite is celebrated during Lent, but not during Mass, since the liturgy of penance is included (#294). A comparison of outlines shows the difference in the rites.

PENITENTIAL RITE (SCRUTINY)	SCRUTINY
For Children	*For Adults*
LITURGY OF THE WORD	LITURGY OF THE WORD
Greeting and Introduction	
Prayer	
Readings	Readings
Homily	Homily
	Invitation to Silent Prayer
Intercessions	Intercessions for the Elect
Exorcism	Exorcism
Anointing with the Oil of Catechumens [or Laying on of Hands]	
Dismissal of the Children	Dismissal of the Elect
LITURGY OF PENANCE	LITURGY OF THE EUCHARIST

Aside from the liturgy of penance being part of the Penitential Rite (Scrutiny), the biggest difference between the adults' and the children's rites is the inclusion of an anointing or laying on of hands in the children's rite. The reason for the anointing being added is unclear. There is no such anointing in the Scrutinies given in Part I. Anointing with the Oil of Catechumens is its own distinct rite for the period of the catechumenate. The anointing seems to be added as "something to do for the elect" right before they are dismissed and the baptized children continue with the liturgy of penance. Is it added as a nice gesture for the elect since they don't "get" the sacrament of penance? The Rite does not give a reason for the anointing or for the difference between Parts I and II.

Another difference between Parts I and II has to do with the exorcism prayer and the laying on of hands. Laying on of hands is an option to be used instead of the anointing. In Part I, the exorcism prayer has two parts; the prayer to the Father, the first person of the Trinity and the second prayer to Jesus Christ. In between the two prayers, the celebrant lays hands on each of the elect. In the children's Penitential Rite (Scrutiny), the exorcism prayer has one part and there is no laying on of hands. Possibly the anointing or laying on of hands was added since there was no laying on of hands in the exorcism prayer.

The exorcism prayer for the children does not contain the rich, poetic language of the adult Scrutinies. Because it is not meant to be celebrated within the Masses of the Third, Fourth and Fifth Sundays of Lent when the Gospels of the Woman at the Well, the Man Born Blind and the Raising of Lazarus are proclaimed, it does not contain the strong images of thirsting, water, darkness, light, death and life that come from the Gospel of John. Consider these excerpts taken from the two exorcism prayers:

PENITENTIAL RITE
(SCRUTINY) (#300)

Loving Father,
free these young people
from whatever could make
  them bad
and help them always to
  walk in your light.
Children:
We want to walk with Jesus,
who gave his life for us.
Help us, Father, to follow
him.

SCRUTINY
(#154)

God of power,
you sent your Son to be our
  Savior.
Grant that these catechumens,
who like the woman of Samaria
thirst for living water,
may turn to the Lord, as they
hear his word and acknowledge
the sins and weaknesses that
weigh them down.

says that the "guidelines given for the adult rite (#141-146) may be followed and adapted, since the children's penitential rites have a similar purpose." The adult rite is a better rite, and I believe that child catechumens are better served celebrating the adult rite than the children's. In addition, most parishes have adult and child catechumens who would celebrate together rather than separately.

The prayer for the adults is much more expressive and convincing. The children's prayer is, in my view, weak and too simple for children of catechetical age. The Scrutinies are not about being "bad," rather they are about the forces of evil from which children need to be freed.

Other differences and inconsistencies exist between the children's rite and the adult Scrutinies. The reason seems to be attributable to the fact that Part II of the Rite was not written by the same committee that wrote Part I and that the authors of Part II of the Rite apparently felt that children needed milder, weaker versions of adult prayers and rituals.[3] My experience with children in the United States, however, strongly suggests that the Rite should be adapted to meet the needs of children who are inquisitive, open, often wise beyond their years, comfortable in large crowds and able to deal with the reality of evil that many of them live with every day of their lives. Language that is flowing and filled with vibrant imagery speaks to children in a way that dull, simple language does not. The vocabulary of the adult prayers is not especially difficult, and children do not have to comprehend every word in order to grasp meaning. What is more important is that they feel the strengthening, healing power of the prayer.

Considering the inconsistencies and awkwardness of the children's Penitential Rite (Scrutiny), I recommend following #291, which

The Scrutinies/Penitential Rites With the Elect and Candidates

Although the Rite says not to combine the elect and candidates for a Scrutiny, pastoral experience shows there are occasions when the elect and candidates can be properly combined in a celebration. A clear distinction must be made between the elect and the candidates. Generally, when the elect and candidates have journeyed together for months or years, separating them for their respective Scrutinies and Penitential Rites seems divisive.

Preparing for the Scrutiny

Once again, the readings and prayers of the rite itself provide the basis for the preparation session. Each of the respective Scrutinies has vivid images that help the children "progress in their perception of sin and their desire for salvation" (#143). The prayers and readings are filled with images of Jesus Christ as living water, light of the world, resurrection and life (First, Second and Third Scrutinies, respectively). Thirsting/dryness and water, blindness/darkness and light, death/bondage and life/freedom are images that can help children relate to the realities of good and evil. By reflecting on the images found in the readings and prayers, the children come to a sense of their own struggle in a world that is filled with powers, structures and systems that oppress them.

Sample Session

A Preparation Session for a Scrutiny

This sample preparation session uses the images that emerge from the prayers and readings of the Second Scrutiny (celebrated on the Fourth Sunday of Lent). This session would take place on the Third Sunday of Lent after the breaking open of the word. Or, it could be adapted and expanded as a day of recollection.

- Gathering and Introduction
- My Story and God's Story
- Reflection on Darkness
- Connecting With the Rite
- Closing Ritual

Gathering and Introduction

Families, sponsors, godparents and companions join the elect and candidates. Adult elect and adult candidates may also be present. This is a good session to have all the elect and candidates together. Appropriate adaptations are made to accommodate the adult elect and candidates. Greet and welcome everyone. Begin with a simple opening prayer. Then ask one of the catechumens or candidates to describe the highlights of the breaking open of the word to those who just joined them. Recall with the group that the season of Lent is a time for purification and enlightenment. Bring up some of the themes that were mentioned in the readings and homily of that Sunday. Then move ahead to the upcoming Scrutiny.

My Story and God's Story/Reflection on Darkness

The second and third movements flow together in this guided meditation. The children and adults are asked to remember a time when they were in the dark. As the quiet meditation ends, the second reading from the Fourth Sunday of Lent (Cycle A) is proclaimed. After the meditation, lead a discussion on darkness, particularly what causes darkness in the life of the child. Children are asked to name the things in their lives that cause "darkness" or keep them in the "dark."

The room is dim and preferably carpeted so children and adults can lie on the floor. An enthronement in the middle of the room holds the lectionary and several large, lighted candles.

Invite people to take a comfortable position on the floor or in chairs. Children often do well lying on the floor. Lead the group through a relaxation exercise of deep breathing and muscle stretching. Then, move the group through a guided meditation. Children as well as adults participate.

Catechist: I invite you to close your eyes and walk with me through an imagination exercise.

First, welcome Jesus into your heart. Talk with Jesus for a little while, and tell Jesus how you are feeling today.

Invite Jesus to come and walk with you now. You and Jesus are walking down a road. The road is lined with trees. Imagine yourself on the road with Jesus and anyone else you want to be there; maybe a parent, a godparent, a friend, or just you and Jesus.

(Silence)

It's early evening and it is starting to get dark as you walk down the road. You stop at a grassy hill and sit down with Jesus. The sky has become dark. The darkness is all around you. You are not afraid because Jesus is with you. But you start to think about the things that do scare you. Talk to Jesus about anything that scares you.

(Silence)

Maybe things at home. At school. In the world.

(Silence)

Talk to Jesus about yourself, now. There are things outside of us that we don't like, that "scare" us. Is there anything inside you that you need to change or work on? Tell Jesus about that now.

(Silence)

Finally, talk with Jesus about the good parts you see in yourself. Tell Jesus about those parts of yourself.

When you are finished talking to Jesus, you look up and see the bright moon and millions of stars. You feel as though you are surrounded by light.

Listen, now, to a reading from the Letter of Paul to the Ephesians.

Read Ephesians 5:8-14 (Fourth Sunday of Lent, Cycle A).

In small groups or in the large group ask the elect and candidates to share some of the things they told Jesus. What in the world scares them? What in themselves scares them? After the elect and candidates respond, others may share their thoughts.

Incorporate the children's and adult's responses into a litany as an adaptation of the intercessions in the Scrutiny.

Connecting With the Rite

Make reference to the upcoming Scrutiny being a time when the community will pray for the elect and candidates. It is a time when the community prays that God will take away the darkness and that Jesus will be their light.

Catechist: How has the parish community's prayer helped you in the past? How can the parish's prayer help you now?

Closing Ritual

Pray one of the minor exorcisms given for the Period of the Catechumenate (#94).

Rehearsing for the Scrutiny

By this time, parents and godparents may be comfortable with celebrating the rites with the Sunday assembly. A "walk through" may or may not be necessary.

Reflection Session After the Scrutiny

The unpacking of the rite has now become a familiar and comfortable process for the children. In most cases "How did you feel?" and "What did it mean?" have become welcome opportunities for the children and others to share.

Other Options

It is preferable to hold a preparation session before each Scrutiny. After the elect have celebrated and then reflected on one Scrutiny, they should spend some time preparing for the upcoming Scrutiny. However, a full preparation session may not be possible before each Scrutiny because they are celebrated on three consecutive Sundays. If there is not time for a group preparation session, godparents, sponsors and/or catechists may spend time talking individually or in small groups with the elect about the dryness (First Scrutiny), darkness (Second

Scrutiny) and death (Third Scrutiny) in their lives. They should also discuss the strengths and goodness in their lives that need to be strengthened.

You can approach the question of evil and good in the life of a child in many different ways. How the question is asked depends on the maturity of the child and your own personal style. The purpose of the question is to help the child recognize and name the weakness and evil that need to be eliminated and the good that needs to be strengthened.

Here are some questions I ask children in preparation for a Scrutiny. You may talk with children differently. I would generally ask only one or two of the questions, depending on the child or the group of children. The questions need to be put in the context of the lectionary reading for the respective Scrutiny. And, as always, the examples need to be adapted to the age, maturity and needs of the children as well as to your own style.

- What scares you?
- What is your scariest nightmare?
- What are you afraid of?
- What is something that you really need or you are longing for?
- What part of you hurts and needs to be healed?
- What can God help you with so you can become a better person?
- What part of you feels dried-up or lifeless? (First Scrutiny)
- What causes you to feel dark or hurt? (Second Scrutiny)
- Where do things feel dead or lifeless in your home, school or group? (Third Scrutiny)
- In what ways are you strong?
- What brings light/happiness to your life?
- Name one of your best qualities.

The last three questions get at what is "upright, strong, and good" (#141) in the elect.

The community will pray that these qualities be strengthened. Whether you ask these questions in the context of a meditation or in an individual conversation, time spent preparing the children for a Scrutiny will enhance the celebration and allow them to participate more fruitfully.

The Sacrament of Penance for Baptized Candidates

Related to the celebration of Scrutinies and Penitential Rites is the question of when baptized candidates celebrate the Sacrament of Penance.

Baptized children who are candidates for reception into full communion with the Roman Catholic Church are to celebrate the Sacrament of Penance prior to their reception into the Church (National Statute 36). Children who are baptized Catholics would also celebrate the Sacrament of Penance prior to the reception of Confirmation and Eucharist in accord with canons 914, 988 and 989.

The celebration of penance is to be seen as an occasion of grace for those who desire or need the sacrament, not as a strict requirement. Children who are not conscious of serious sin are not required to receive the sacrament, although they are to receive formation and catechesis for the Sacrament of Reconciliation and learn of opportunities to celebrate the sacrament.[4]

Baptized children may wish to celebrate the sacrament at a parish penance service, or they may wish to see a priest privately prior to the celebration of Confirmation and Eucharist. Catechists and the initiation coordinator may assist those children and families who wish to receive the sacrament.

Unbaptized children do not receive the Sacrament of Penance prior to Baptism because Baptism, the door to all the sacraments, must be received before any of the other sacraments. The Sacrament of Penance does not concern itself with prebaptismal sins, but only those committed after Baptism. However, catechumens may benefit from some formation and catechesis for the Sacrament of Penance. After initiation, their continuing religious formation would at some point include sacramental catechesis for penance.

The Presentations and Children

After the celebration of the Scrutinies, the Presentations of the Creed and the Lord's Prayer take place, "unless for pastoral reasons, they have been anticipated during the period of the catechumenate" (#147). The Creed is presented to the children during the week following the First Scrutiny (#148) and the Lord's Prayer is presented during the week following the Third Scrutiny or on Holy Saturday (#149).

The children celebrate the presentations at the same time the adult elect receive the Creed and Lord's Prayer. Or, if a group of their peers is gathering during the week, the presentations may be celebrated with a group of the children's companions. This provides an opportunity for the elect to be with their baptized peers. For example, if children in the parish are gathering for Lenten prayer, the presentations might be celebrated at that time. Or, if the elect are students at the Catholic school, the presentations may be done during the week with their peers at school. Since the presentations are minor rites, they do not necessarily have to be celebrated with the Sunday assembly.

As with the adults, the children are to commit to memory the Creed and the Lord's Prayer. Parents, godparents and/or sponsors help the children memorize the prayers and talk with the children about how these prayers have been important in their lives. They can also talk with the children about the meaning and significance of the prayers. You should provide parents, godparents and sponsors with materials that will help them talk with their children about these ancient prayers. A reflection session on the prayers is offered after each of the presentations.

Lastly, the children may receive the Lord's Prayer on Holy Saturday, particularly if that is when the adults celebrate the final presentation. In anticipation of the Easter Vigil, the children likewise participate in the other preparation rites that are celebrated on Holy Saturday (#185-205).

Celebration of the Sacraments of Initiation

The children's celebration of the sacraments of initiation preferably takes place at the Easter Vigil (#256, 304, National Statute 18). The paschal nature of the sacraments of initiation is brought out most fully and completely at the Easter Vigil. The rhythm and flow of the initiation journey culminates most fruitfully when the children are part of the high point of the liturgical year, the Easter Vigil.

Although some would argue that the Vigil is too long and complex for children, my experience and the experience of many others suggest just the opposite. Children relish the rich sights, sounds, smells and feel of the Vigil. They are taken in by the grandeur of the new fire, the paschal candle, the processions and the Exultet. The Sacred Scriptures proclaimed in dark and in light, with passion and reverence, with song and acclamation, envelop and enthrall the children. The awesomeness of being plunged into gushing waters, being smeared with greasy and fragrant oils, being fed with hearty bread and rich wine speaks to children about the paschal mystery in a way that no other celebration can. So, despite the lateness or earliness of the hour, the Vigil is a celebration for children and adults to which none other can compare.

Sacraments of Initiation With Baptized Peers

Despite the great preference for initiation at the Easter Vigil, the Rite makes additional comments regarding when children are to celebrate the sacraments. Paragraph 256 first says that the celebration of the initiation preferably takes place at the Vigil. Then, the paragraph continues by saying that the celebration of the sacraments "must also be consistent with the program of catechetical instruction they are receiving, since the candidates should, if possible, come to the sacraments of initiation at the time that their baptized companions are to receive Confirmation or Eucharist."

Similarly, #304 and #308 make the same assertions: The celebration of the sacraments of initiation preferably takes place at the Easter Vigil (#304), and the baptized companions "may be completing their Christian initiation in the sacraments of Confirmation and the Eucharist at this same celebration" (#308). This seems to be a mixed message. First, the preference is given for the children to celebrate the sacraments of initiation at the Easter Vigil. Then, the statement is made that they should celebrate "at the time" their companions celebrate Confirmation and Eucharist.

Several questions and possibilities arise as a result of this wording. First, does this mean that baptized children of the catechetical group celebrate Confirmation and Eucharist at the Easter Vigil with the children who are being

baptized? This seems to be the case, especially since #308 refers to baptized children completing their initiation "at this same celebration," and does not specify whether it is the Vigil or another time. Likewise, #309-329, "Celebration of the Sacraments of Initiation," make reference to "baptized children of the catechetical group" completing their initiation when the elect are baptized. This section refers to the celebration being at the Vigil, and it refers to baptized peers. "Baptized children of the catechetical group" are being confirmed (#322) and receiving the Eucharist for the first time (#329). There is also the possibility that even if an entire catechetical group did not necessarily complete their initiation at the Vigil, baptized children who served as companions or as part of a sponsoring family might complete their initiation. Paragraph 308 also says that the bishop "should grant the faculty to confirm such children to the priest who will be the celebrant."

Another possibility could be that the phrase "at the time that their baptized companions are to receive Confirmation and Eucharist" (#256) refers to the general liturgical time of Easter. Paragraph 256 refers to the unbaptized children being "admitted to the sacraments at Easter." Here, the elect would be initiated at the Easter Vigil and their baptized peers would celebrate Confirmation and Eucharist later in the Easter season. Then, there would be the consistency of initiation during the Easter season. This interpretation would address those who might want to fully initiate the unbaptized children in one season of the liturgical year and then complete the initiation of the baptized children at another season of the year.

A third and least desirable possibility is that the elect would celebrate the sacraments of initiation at a time other than the Easter Vigil; that is, when their baptized companions receive Confirmation and Eucharist. This interpretation is made in light of the fact that several times the Rite refers to the possibility of the celebration of the sacraments of initiation being at a time other than the Easter Vigil (#8, 256, 304, 306). Likewise, #309-329, "Celebration of the Sacraments of Initiation," are written such that the initiation of children could be at a time other than the Vigil (#309-311).

Notwithstanding all of the above, Part I of the Rite (#8), states that "the Easter Vigil should be regarded as the proper time for the sacraments of initiation." Every effort should be made to see that children are afforded that same opportunity as adults to celebrate their initiation at the Easter Vigil.

Celebrating the Sacraments of Initiation With Children

Reference has already been made to #304-329 in the Rite, "Celebration of the Sacraments of Initiation With Children." We can see many difference between the rites as adapted for children and the adult rite given in Part I (#218-243).

The biggest difference is that although both versions allow for celebration of initiation at the Easter Vigil or outside the Vigil, the rite adapted for children is written as if the celebration were outside the Vigil. For example, the Outline of the Rite for children does not include the Service of Light, Litany of Saints, or Renewal of Baptismal Promises (At the Easter Vigil). Furthermore, paragraph 309 describes children, families and parishioners gathering as "Mass" begins, with no mention of the Vigil. One presumes the adaptation is written differently for children so that it can be used at a time other than the Vigil.

The children's adaptation also includes baptized children of the catechetical group completing their initiation, whereas the adult rite in Part I does not include the initiation of

baptized candidates. A combined rite for adults, "Celebration at the Easter Vigil of the Sacraments of Initiation and of the Rite of Reception into Full Communion of the Catholic Church" is provided later in Part II.

Most of the other differences between the rite of initiation for adults and the adaptation for children are related to the celebration being allowed outside of the Vigil or the inclusion of baptized candidates of the catechetical group. For example, in the adaptation for children, there is an optional "Community's Profession of Faith" (#312) as part of the celebration of Baptism. The community is invited to profess its faith by reciting the Apostles' Creed or Nicene Creed. This is most likely included as an alternative to the Renewal of Baptismal Promises that takes place at the Easter Vigil. If the celebration of the sacraments of initiation for children is at the Vigil, the Renewal of Baptismal Promises would be used instead of the Community's Profession of Faith. Although the Rite does not make specific mention, the Community's Profession of Faith is an option for celebration outside of the Vigil.

The Children's Profession of Faith also contains an optional "Anointing With the Oil of Catechumens." Paragraph 315 says that if the children have not been anointed previously, they are to be anointed at this time, prior to their profession of faith. The Rite goes on to say, however, that "ordinarily this rite is omitted... (see # 33.7)." The anointing should generally take place at the Pentential Rite (Scrutiny), rather than during the celebration of the sacraments of initiation.

Once again, the differences between the adult rite and the adaptation for children reinforce the fact that Part II is indeed an adaptation of the norm given in Part I. When there is doubt or question, rely on Part I.

Confirmation and Children of Catechetical Age

The Rite clearly states that when children of catechetical age are baptized they are also to be confirmed (#305, National Statutes 14, 18, 19). Moreover, the Rite strongly states that "adults are not to be baptized without receiving confirmation immediately afterward, unless some serious reason stands in the way" (#215). Since children of catechetical age are considered adults for the purpose of Christian initiation (canon 852.1, National Statute 18), they, too, are to be confirmed.

Canon law also clearly states, "Unless a grave reason prevents it, an adult who is baptized is to be confirmed immediately after Baptism and participate in the celebration of the Eucharist, also receiving Communion."[5] Once again, "adult" includes children of catechetical age, therefore children are to be confirmed at the time of their Baptism. Furthermore, the Rite reiterates this in National Statute 14 by saying the children are to receive all three sacraments of initiation, "whether at the Easter Vigil or, if necessary, at some other time." Thus, "the interrelation or coalescence" of Baptism, Confirmation and Eucharist is to be maintained even if the children are baptized outside the Easter Vigil.

Even though the Rite of Christian Initiation of Adults and the Code of Canon Law are emphatic about the unity of Baptism, Confirmation and Eucharist, baptizing children of catechetical age, but delaying Confirmation—and Eucharist as well—continues to be common practice. There are different versions of this anomaly. In some parishes, it is the practice to baptize children of catechetical age at the Easter Vigil (or at another time) and welcome them to the table for Eucharist, but delay their Confirmation until the time their peers who were baptized as infants are confirmed. Or, in other cases,

especially when children are seven or eight years old and their peers who were baptized as infants are preparing for First Eucharist, the parish baptizes the child, but delays Confirmation and Eucharist so the child "can receive Eucharist with her or his group" and be confirmed "with her or his group."

In both these scenarios, the reason given for delaying Confirmation or Eucharist is that the candidate needs or wants to receive Confirmation and/or Eucharist with the baptized peer group. And, the reasoning continues, if the candidate receives Baptism, Confirmation and Eucharist, he or she will "be ahead of" or "out of step with" the rest of the group. She or he will not "fit into" the regular parish religious education program. Those who argue for the delay of Confirmation and/or Eucharist claim pastoral discretion warrants the delay. They believe receiving a sacrament with a catechetical peer group or "fitting into" the religious education program is sufficient reason to disrupt the fullness of sacramental initiation.

I disagree. A peer-group celebration or a religious education program is not a "grave reason" to prevent a child from receiving full Christian initiation.[6] Often, celebrating Confirmation or Eucharist with a peer group is more of an issue for parents or for parish religious educators than it is for the children. If some children do feel strongly about celebrating with the rest of their peers, then they may still take part in the later celebrations of Confirmation and Eucharist. While a child cannot be confirmed a second time, he or she can still be present at the celebration. And a child can certainly receive Eucharist with those receiving their first Eucharist.

Children who are fully initiated still need to participate in religious education programs even though they are fully initiated. If, however, a parish offers only sacramental preparation for a particular age group (for example, the only eighth-grade catechetical offering is sacramental preparation for Confirmation), that parish needs to broaden the catechetical offerings it has for young people. A sound catechetical program is more than sacramental preparation. A complete parish catechetical program offers ongoing religious formation for the baptized (those fully initiated and those baptized in infancy) and sacramental catechesis for those preparing to celebrate a sacrament. In other words, sacramental catechesis should be separate and distinct from religious education.

Another reason that pastoral ministers or parents give for delaying Confirmation is that they feel the candidate is ready for Baptism but is not "ready" for Confirmation or does not "fully understand" the meaning of Confirmation. Catechists and pastoral ministers often say to me, "I think the child is ready for Baptism but not Confirmation. She or he doesn't really understand the Holy Spirit and what Confirmation is."

First of all, being ready for a sacrament is not a matter of understanding the sacrament. One can mentally "understand" a sacrament and not be ready for it. Second, readiness for Confirmation entails readiness for initiation, which means conversion. If the child has experienced conversion, she or he is ready for initiation: Baptism, Confirmation and Eucharist. Thus, if a child is not ready for Confirmation, he or she cannot possibly be ready for Baptism. Confirmation cannot be seen as separate from Baptism.

A third reason given for delaying Confirmation or Eucharist is that parents will object to some children "getting" all three sacraments at one celebration, while children baptized in infancy have to wait and "do a lot more work" to "get" Confirmation and Eucharist. My response to parents or pastoral ministers who raise this objection is to point out that they are correct. The Church does

have different ways of initiating children. And, though there seem to be inconsistencies between the two, there are two ways to be fully initiated. Some children are baptized in infancy with Confirmation and Eucharist delayed. Other children and adults are fully initiated at one celebration. Isn't the diversity of our tradition rich and wonderful!

Proper information and education for the parish regarding sacramental initiation helps avert and soften such controversies. I find that most parishioners are agreeable and amenable to the fact that children are initiated differently when the reasons and rationale have been properly explained. They are happy that a child and family are coming to the Church. If a person or family is interested in full initiation for children of catechetical age, I might talk to them about being sponsors and/or the possibility of their children completing their initiation with the catechumens.

Lastly, insofar as confirming a child immediately after Baptism, some priests and initiation ministers are hesitant to have a priest confirm a child. However, canon law and the Rite of Christian Initiation of Adults are once again clear that priests who baptize adults do have the faculty of administering Confirmation by the law itself. According to canon 883.2:

> The following have the faculty of administering confirmation by the law itself: with regard to the person in question, the presbyter who by reason of office or mandate of the diocesan bishop baptizes one who is no longer an infant or one already baptized whom he admits into full communion with the Catholic Church.[7]

In other words, the priest who baptizes "one who is no longer an infant" also confirms that person. And National Statute 14 states that the celebration of Baptism, Confirmation and Eucharist can be outside the Vigil, if necessary. Likewise, when a baptized child is brought into full communion with the Roman Catholic Church, she or he is also to be confirmed. National Statute 35 says, "The Confirmation of such candidates for reception should not be deferred, nor should they be admitted to the Eucharist until they are confirmed."

In addition, canon 885.2 says that "a presbyter who has this faculty must use it for those in whose favor the faculty was granted." In other words, the priest who has the faculty must confirm a child of catechetical age when he or she is baptized or brought into full communion. If a bishop wants to confirm all adults and children of catechetical age, he must "reserve to himself the baptism of adults in accord with canon 863" (National Statute, 13). If the bishop wants to confirm children of catechetical age, he has to baptize and confirm all adults (including children of catechetical age). There is little chance that any bishop will baptize and confirm all candidates for initiation. Here is the key to the presbyters' faculty to confirm. Although the "diocesan bishop is the proper minister of the sacraments of initiation for adults, including children of catechetical age" (National Statute 11) if he does not intend to baptize, and thus confirm all adults, then the priest baptizes and confirms adults and children of catechetical age.

Clearly, then, children of catechetical age are to be confirmed and celebrate Eucharist when they are baptized. They are to be confirmed whether the presider is priest or bishop and whether the celebration is at the Easter Vigil or at another time.

Summary

The three sacraments of initiation closely combine to bring children to Christ's "full stature" and enable them "to carry out the mission of the entire people of God in the Church and in the world" (*RCIA*, General Introduction, #2). Through sacramental initiation, the children become disciples of Jesus. The Easter Vigil is the peak moment in the journey of conversion that leads to full discipleship. At the Vigil, they are washed and created anew by the waters of baptism; they are anointed and configured to the likeness of Christ Jesus by the sacred chrism; finally they are welcomed to the table and are nourished by the flesh and blood of God's own Son.

The period of purification and enlightenment was their final preparation for this climactic celebration. Through a process of liturgical catechesis, the Scrutinies and presentations provided the basis for the forty-day Lenten retreat that preceded initiation at the Easter Vigil. Their conversion completed by the Scrutinies, the children are fully initiated and make their transition into the body of the faithful. The journey continues.

REFERENCES

[1] Dick Westley, *Morality and Its Beyond* (Mystic, Conn.: Twenty-Third Publications, 1984), p. 32.

[2] Although the divorce or separation of parents is often necessary, it causes anxiety for most children. It often leads to questions about security and stability, at least temporarily.

[3] Robert D. Duggan, pastor of St. Rose of Lima Parish in Gaithersburg, Maryland, and a team member of the North American Forum on the Catechumenate, has studied the original Latin text of the *Rite of Christian Initiation of Adults* and has done extensive research and work with the document. His doctoral dissertation from The Catholic University of America was a study of conversion in the *Rite of Christian Initiation of Adults*. According to Duggan, the committee that wrote Part I of the Rite did not write Part II. The rites in Part II do not have the depth and thoroughness of Part I. For example, the section on children of catechetical age has nothing to say about the first three periods of initiation, but it does contain one short paragraph on the period of mystagogy. There is also only one Penitential Rite (Scrutiny) given for children, whereas three are given for adults.

[4] *Code of Canon Law*. See commentary on canon 914, p. 653.

[5] *Code of Canon Law*, canon 866.

[6] Ibid. Canon 842 states Baptism, Confirmation and Eucharist are required for full Christian initiation.

[7] The commentary on canon 883.2 in the *Code of Canon Law*, p. 635, describes the office of the priest who baptizes (or admits to full communion) one who is no longer an infant "as generally that of pastor, parochial vicar, rector of a church, chaplain, indeed any priest with some pastoral office."

6

The Period of Postbaptismal Catechesis or Mystagogy

On the Second Sunday of Easter, the neophytes gathered in their regular place, upstairs in the parish hall. Child neophytes, adult neophytes, parents, spouses, godparents, sponsors and companions were present. The neophytes were sharing their feelings and reaction to the Easter Vigil. The discussion was focused for the moment on the waters of baptism. Fourteen-year-old Neil described how he felt when the baptismal water was gushing over him. Neil said, "For just a second, I was really scared. When Father Joe had a hold of my head and the water just kept coming, I lost my breath. It was like the first time I was in the ocean and the current swept me under. I thought I was gonna drown."

Everyone in the room nodded in agreement. A brief, yet pregnant moment of silence followed. Neil made a very direct connection between the power of water and the mystery of baptism. There was an unspoken understanding that something of each person had "drowned" and come up out of the water made new.

Neil's story spoke volumes about the mystery of Baptism without a catechist "teaching" or instructing the initiates. The period of postbaptismal catechesis, or mystagogy, is a time for the neophytes (the newly initiated) to reflect upon the experience of sacramental initiation and "to grow in deepening their grasp of the paschal mystery" (#244). The neophytes have experienced the mystery of Baptism, Confirmation and Eucharist, and now they spend time "making it part of their lives" (#244). The term *mystagogy* refers to mystery and is a time for unpacking "a fuller and more effective understanding" of the mysteries of faith (#245).

The Rite outlines how the neophytes are to make the mysteries part of their lives. In regard to children who are neophytes, one small paragraph in Part II (#330) says that the guidelines given for adults are to be adapted for children. In addition, the paragraph says that "their companions" are to be included in the postbaptismal catechesis.

Reflecting on the Paschal Mystery

The paschal mystery is most fully and marvelously encountered in the Eucharist. Thus, the primary context for the entire period of mystagogy is the Eucharist. More specifically, the Rite describes several ways that the neophytes, along with the faithful, grow in their understanding of the paschal mystery. They do this by:

- meditating on the Gospel;
- sharing in the Eucharist;
- doing works of charity;
- reflecting on "their experience of the sacraments they have received."

Let's take a look at each of the "ways to understanding."

Meditating on the Gospel

The neophytes celebrate the Sunday eucharistic liturgies of the Easter season with their families and with the entire local community. By participating in the Eucharist, they hear the Gospel proclaimed, and the homilist helps them to "meditate" further on its meaning. Robert D. Duggan points out that the homilist has a weighty responsibility during the period of mystagogy. The homilist has the chief responsibility for mystagogical catechesis. "The classic examples of mystagogical catechesis are episcopal homilies delivered during Easter week."[1] The readings from Cycle A are "particularly suitable" for the neophytes and may be used "even when Christian initiation is celebrated outside the usual times" (#247).

In other words, mystagogy happens primarily at Sunday Mass through regular participation in the Eucharist. Your efforts during this period need to be concentrated on working with the homilist to ensure good homilies for the neophytes and the entire community. It is most helpful, of course, if the homilist knows the neophytes and their families. If the homilist doesn't know the children and their families well, you should talk with the homilist about the progress of the neophytes.

Sharing in the Eucharist

Secondly, the entire eucharistic celebration helps the neophytes deepen their grasp of the paschal mystery. By fully participating in the mystery of Eucharist, children will enter more deeply into it. One cannot "explain" the paschal mystery to children. Children have to be a part of it, and sharing in the Eucharist is the principal way one participates in the paschal mystery. Sharing in the Eucharist allows the children to taste, eat and drink the paschal mystery, but it also enables them to experience the paschal mystery through the assembly, the embodiment of the Risen Christ. And now the children are part of that Body. Standing together on Sunday morning with the worshipping assembly, the neophytes receive the highest form of mystagogical catechesis possible. For they hear the word, they meditate on its meaning, they drink the blood and eat the body, and they are one with the Body of Christ. This is far more meaningful than any post-Easter "class" that explains the meaning of the sacraments.

Doing Works of Charity

A third way the Rite says that the neophytes can grow in their understanding of the paschal mystery is by "doing works of charity." This is how we live the paschal mystery. Living and working as a follower of Jesus connects the child in some way to the great mystery of Jesus' life. To give of self for the benefit of others is following the path of Jesus.

Children primarily do their "works of charity" in the home and school since that is where most of their time is spent. Through their daily acts of self-giving and kindness to family and classmates, they participate in the paschal mystery. Although it may sound simplistic, being generous, thoughtful, patient and compassionate to sisters, brothers and parents is not always an easy task for children.

Being open, nonjudgmental, courteous, fair and self-giving at school is not always easy either.

On the Fourth Sunday of Easter at St. Margaret Parish, one mother testified to the Sunday assembly that her daughter, Alicia, "loved coming to church on Sundays" and was being helpful around the house by reading to her younger sister at bedtime. Alicia's relatively small act of charity was a big help to her mother and a way of giving of herself.

Reflecting on the Easter Vigil and the Sacraments of Initiation

In addition to meditating on the Gospel, sharing in the Eucharist and doing works of charity, neophytes come to a "fuller and more effective understanding" of mystery "above all through their experience of the sacraments they have received" (#245). This means that receiving the sacraments in and of themselves deepens their understanding of the paschal mystery. I suggest that it also means that by reflecting on their experience of sacramental initiation they can deepen their grasp of the paschal mystery.

The Easter Vigil and the celebration of the sacraments of initiation are such profound and rich experiences that children need time to unpack and explore the meaning of what has happened. Mystagogy means reflecting on the mysteries. It means delving into the mystery that one has experienced in order to discover its fullness. The process of liturgical catechesis (preparing for, celebrating and reflecting on the liturgy) continues to be used with the children to explore the depth and breadth of the mystery that has become a part of their lives. By reflecting on the Vigil, children come to see more clearly how they have become one with the living God and the Christian community.

In order to do this, a parish mystagogue, a specially trained catechist, should lead the children and their families in mystagogical sessions. A mystagogue helps children connect the mystery to their everyday lives, just as Neil connected the baptismal washing to his experience of nearly drowning in the ocean. The symbols of the sacraments and all that surrounded them in the Easter Vigil are the context for the mystagogical reflection sessions. Depending on the neophytes and the approach of the mystagogue, several sessions might be needed in order to unpack the fullness of the bathing, the anointing, the meal, the light and dark, the assembly, the Scripture readings of the Vigil.

A sample of one type of mystagogical session, using the liturgical catechesis method, is outlined below. This session could take place on the Second Sunday of Easter after the neophytes and their families celebrated Mass with the Sunday assembly. Or, it could take place at another time, such as a weeknight during Easter week. The session might also include adult neophytes with their godparents and sponsors.

Sample Session

- Gathering and Introduction
- My Story and God's Story
- Reflection on the Vigil
- Connecting With the Vigil
- Closing Ritual

Gathering and Introduction

Neophytes, families, godparents, sponsors and companions gather on the Second Sunday of Easter.

A paschal candle, the lectionary, a large glass bowl full of water, a large vessel full of oil, and bread and wine are enthroned. During the gathering time, pictures from Holy

Saturday are available for the children and families. (Pictures should not be taken during the liturgy, but discreetly before and after it.) Allow ample time for mingling and talking about the pictures.

My Story and God's Story

Begin with a reading from one of the Sunday Masses of the Easter season. There are connections between the readings from the Vigil and the readings for the Masses of the Easter season.

Read John 20:19-21 from the Gospel for the Second Sunday of Easter, Cycle A. Allow time for silence.

Mystagogue: After the "first Easter," Jesus' disciples gathered behind locked doors, not sure of what was happening. How do you think they were feeling? What was going on in their minds? *(Pause for responses.)*

We gather here today certain of what has happened. Jesus rose from the dead! Yet, at the same time, you may be feeling some uncertainty or questions or maybe just outright joy. Let's talk a little bit about what you have been feeling this past week since your Baptism, Confirmation and Eucharist.

How do you feel now that you [your child] are fully initiated into God's family?

How did you feel throughout this past week?

Reflection on the Vigil

The mystagogue invites the group to remember the Easter Vigil. The mystagogue leads a guided meditation, walking through the highlights of the Vigil. The reflection allows time for the neophytes, parents, godparents, sponsors and companions to remember how they felt during the Vigil and what the highlights of the Vigil were for them.

Connecting With the Vigil

The mystagogue invites the children first, then the parents, godparents, sponsors and companions to talk about their experience of the Vigil. The mystagogue may ask, "What stands out for you about the Easter Vigil? How did you feel?"

Depending on the size of the group, this may take the remainder of the hour or two in which the group is gathering. According to what the children say and how they respond, further mystagogical sessions are designed to unpack the most significant aspects of the Vigil that the children identify, such as the water bath, the chrismation, the reception of communion, the new fire.

If time allows, the mystagogue picks up on the responses given and helps the children understand the meaning of their sacramental experiences.

Eleven-year-old Amanda said she remembered being cold standing outside in the dark, in the rain, and then she said how good it felt to walk into the church with everybody singing. It made her feel "tingly." The mystagogue later came back to Amanda's response and asked her and the group, "What did that mean to have everybody walk into the church with you?"

Amanda and the rest of the group talked more about the meaning of walking into the church.

Closing Ritual

The closing ritual hearkens back to the Vigil.

The mystagogue invites the group to stand and come to the water. While a suitable song from the Vigil is sung, the neophytes and their parent and godparents come to the water. Parents and godparents sprinkle the neophytes with the water.

There are other ways the children can reflect on their experience of the sacraments. There could be a mystagogical session on each of the sacraments. In these sessions, the sacramental symbols would be "cracked open." Or, a more casual approach could be used. Godparents, or parents, could talk with the neophytes about their experience of sacramental initiation. They would ask the child questions like the ones given in the sample session. The initiation team would need to provide support materials to help godparents with the exercise.

Mystagogical catechesis flows from the experience of sacramental initiation and continues to be based on the Sunday eucharistic liturgy. It is a kind of liturgical catechesis because the point of departure is the rite of initiation and its "setting" is the Sunday Masses of Easter Season, which the Rite calls the "Neophyte Masses."

Consequently, the initiation team need not be concerned with the question, "How do we get them to come back for sessions after Easter?" The question is rather, "How will the liturgies of the Easter season help the young neophytes deepen their grasp of the paschal mystery and grow as faithful disciples?" That is not to say that there are no postbaptismal catechetical sessions after Easter. One was suggested above. Likewise, National Statute 24 states that there are to be monthly gatherings of neophytes for at least one year. However, the primary context of the catechesis is not "more classes" after Easter. In reality, after any big climactic experience, there is a period of "letdown," and neophytes are often not inclined to come back for classes.[2] But they do come on Sunday and worship with the community of the faithful.

The Mystagogue and Children

The mystagogue is the person in the parish who helps the children unpack the mystery into which they have been incorporated. The mystagogue leads the reflection sessions after the Easter Vigil. Or, the mystagogue may talk with children individually or in their families to help them unpack the meaning of the most sacred Christian mysteries.

What is most important is that the mystagogue is a person who has a sense of mystery and appreciates children's affinity to mystery. The mystagogue is a person who sees mystery in the birth of a baby, the laughter of a toddler, the playfulness of a preschooler, the imagination of a young child and the chaos of an adolescent. Likewise, the mystagogue is one who stands in awe at the power of a thunderstorm or the beauty of a freshly plowed field. The mystagogue is one who stands in awe of life itself. He or she is a person who lives life to the fullest and sees the paschal mystery present in everyday living. Such a person can relate to a child who is delighted and fascinated by being "greased" at the Easter Vigil.

Furthermore, the mystagogue may facilitate the "monthly assemblies" of neophytes that extend for a year after their initiation (National Statute 24). These neophyte gatherings may be as simple as coming together after coffee and doughnuts on Sunday or for potluck suppers at a sponsor's home. The mystagogue may invite the children and their families to reflect on the life of discipleship and what it means for their family to share in the mission of Jesus Christ. The mystagogue may also want to address any feelings of "letdown" that are experienced in the weeks and months after the Vigil.

All in all, the mystagogue is one who revels in the mysteries of faith and has the ability to share faith with children. A godparent, sponsor, parent, catechist, pastor or grandparent may serve as mystagogue. Or another person with the necessary sense of mystery may serve solely as the initiation team mystagogue.

Time of Transition

Mystagogy is a time of transition.[3] During mystagogy, children make the transition into the community of the faithful. For some children this may feel like they no longer get the "special attention" of catechumens. In some parishes, the transition from initiation catechesis to "regular" religious education can be stifling for children.

The issue of transition can be addressed in various ways. Some parishes have neophytes sit in a designated place and/or wear their white garments throughout the Easter season (see #248). In this way, they continue to draw special attention after their initiation. Also, if there is to be a Mass with the bishop, children participate in the celebration.

Just as adult neophytes make a transition into their place in the parish, children make a similar transition. Whereas adults may join a Scripture study group or a small faith-sharing community, most parishes primarily have a catechetical program to offer children and youth ministry for adolescents.

Special attention can also be given to children as they make their transition into the "regular" parish catechetical program or youth ministry. The catechetical group may host a welcoming party for children who have been newly initiated, since prior to their initiation catechumens and candidates would not normally be in a parish catechetical program. Likewise, as the children begin their participation in the catechetical program, the catechist needs to be aware that they are neophytes. Ideally, the neophytes would have the opportunity to interact with their catechist and catechetical group prior to regular participation in the program.

Specific attention may be given to the notion of transition. The mystagogue or catechist may facilitate a discussion with young neophytes and their families about times of transitions. For example, children and adolescents experience transition when they:

- cross the street by themselves or go to a friend's house by themselves for the first time;
- start riding a bicycle;
- move from preschool or kindergarten to elementary school;
- move from junior high to high school;
- get a driver's license;
- experience the divorce of their parents;
- grieve the death or loss of a loved one;
- adjust to a new sister or brother;
- get glasses or braces;
- go on their first date or to their first dance;
- stay at home alone for the first time;
- start their first job;
- move to a new home or school.

Here is a sample session on transition that was part of a "neophyte potluck supper" held shortly after Pentecost at the home of one of the godparents. Child and adult neophytes along with their families came to the supper. After social time and supper, the group divided. Adults met together and children together, each having a similar discussion. Those children who were not neophytes were supervised outside by one of the teens present. The length of the children's session was approximately forty minutes.

Sample Session

Gathering

Gather with the children and enter into casual conversation by asking:

- What has it been like to be a fully initiated member of the church?
- How does it feel to be receiving Eucharist?

Allow time for children to talk freely about the questions.

My Story

Move the discussion to the transition the children have been making.

Catechist: Over the past few months, there have been lots of changes in your life. Changes in life are called transitions. A transition is when something or some part of your life is different. For example, when you were a baby you made a transition from crawling to walking. As a walker, you could explore and discover more than you ever had before. There was a whole new world! And, when you made the transition from diapers to training pants, you became much more independent. You no longer needed your mom or dad to change your pants. As you became older and were allowed to go outside by yourself, you once again became even more independent than you were before.

If you had a baby brother or sister born into your family, that was a time of change for your family as you adjusted to the new family member. Or, when you started going to school that was a transition from being at home or at daycare to being on your own at school. There are transitions throughout your life. I'd like you to think quietly now of a transition or change that you remember in your life.

After sufficient quiet time, the children share their story of transition with one another. Depending upon the number of children, this may be done as a large group or in small groups. After the sharing of the stories, you could ask:

- What in your life changed? What was different?
- How did you feel about the change?
- What was good about the change? What was difficult?

The Church's Story

Tell about the time of transition for the apostles and the early Church. After Jesus had left them physically, they had to make a transition to life without Jesus. They had to continue Jesus' mission without him.

Now read from the lectionary or tell the story of the Ascension (Cycle A: Matthew 28:16-20). You should then invite the children's response to the story and provide a brief, age-appropriate explanation.

Catechist: This story happened just after Jesus' resurrection. Jesus was telling his disciples that they must continue his work and ask people from everyplace if they wanted to be disciples. The disciples were used to Jesus' being with them and being their leader. Now, since he was no longer with the disciples physically, he gave the Holy Spirit to them so they could continue his work.

- How do you think the disciples felt when Jesus told them to go out on their own?
- What had changed for the disciples?
- What was good about the change? What was difficult?

Allow time for the children to discuss the questions in the larger group or in smaller groups.

119

Connecting My Story and the Church's Story

Now help the children see that transitions take place in everyone's life. Some transitions are small and others take a lot of courage and adjustment.

Catechist: You have experienced a big transition. When you first began the initiation process you may have known little about God, Jesus and the Church. You became a catechumen or candidate and you experienced many changes in your life as you came to know Jesus better. Now that you are a full member of the Church and a true disciple of Jesus, there are even more changes. You, too, have the responsibility to continue Jesus' work in your home, school and neighborhood. You also have a responsibility to continue learning about God and the Church in our religious education program. You will worship with our community every Sunday. And, like those first disciples, the Holy Spirit will be with you to help and strengthen you.

■ How do you feel about changing from our initiation group sessions to religious education with the other parish children?

■ Since you are a disciple of Jesus, how will you continue his work in your home, school or neighborhood?

Once again, allow time for the children to respond to the questions. Address any questions or concerns the children have.

Closing Ritual

All the children and adults come together for the closing.

Catechist: Neophytes please stand with your parents, godparents and sponsors.

(With hands outstretched over the neophytes the catechist prays:)

God of life,
you raised Jesus Christ from the dead
and promised the gift of everlasting life to all.
Grant that these neophytes,
empowered by your Holy Spirit,
might continue their journey to you
and always be faithful disciples.
We ask this through Christ our Lord.
Amen.

Let us offer one another a sign of peace.

In addition to discussing the neophytes' transition, you should provide each family with information they need to make an easy transition into the parish catechetical program. The director of religious education and/or coordinator of youth ministry may wish to meet with the neophytes and their families to talk about the continuing formation of the child neophyte.

Continuing Catechetical Formation

Once the children have been fully initiated and have become part of the community of the faithful, they have a need for continuing catechetical formation. Most parish catechetical programs for children are religious education for baptized children, though there are certainly exceptions. Catechumens and candidates do not usually participate in programs designed for the baptized. Their formation happens in the process of initiation.

Once the "formal" process of initiation has ended, however, the neophytes are incorporated into the parish catechetical program. Like all the baptized, the neophytes have a need for ongoing formation that will nourish their life of faith. Their journey of conversion continues, and conversion includes deepening one's understanding of the faith and one's relationship with God through catechetical formation.

The neophytes participate in the same catechetical formation program as their previously baptized peers. Some parents and religious educators are concerned that the neophytes will be "ahead of" or "out of step" with their peers because the neophytes have already received Confirmation and/or Eucharist. Others worry that neophytes will be "behind" their peers because the neophytes have not had years of "formal" religious education.[4] In order to address these concerns, you must take a look at the parish catechetical program.

If indeed the program is religious education and/or catechesis for the baptized, then the neophytes and those baptized as infants both benefit from the instruction and formation that informs their faith and nourishes their relationship with God. Although the neophytes are fully initiated, like their previously baptized peers, their catechetical needs do not end with the sacraments. The questions and concerns of the neophytes change as they mature and grow in the Christian life, just like those of their peers. All children, neophytes and those baptized in infancy, need developmentally appropriate religious education and catechesis to meet their ever-changing needs.

Sometimes a parish catechetical program may not fit the needs of neophytes. If a parish has a particular grade level or age group that is solely sacramental preparation, rather than catechetical formation, the sacramental preparation is not appropriate for neophytes. In other words, if "second-grade religious education" is in reality "second-grade Eucharist preparation" or if "eighth-grade religious education" is in reality "eighth-grade Confirmation preparation," then this is not acceptable for a second-grade or eighth-grade neophyte.

In these cases, the parish must examine the difference between sacramental catechesis and religious education. Children who desire and are "ready" to prepare for Confirmation and Eucharist participate in sacramental catechesis, whereas all baptized children have a need for ongoing religious education. An effective parish catechetical program includes sacramental catechesis for candidates who are preparing for a particular sacrament and ongoing religious education/formation for all children and adults.

It is important to make the distinction between sacramental catechesis and religious education. Not only will a parish's catechetical efforts be more holistic when sacramental catechesis is separate from and complementary to religious education, but neophytes will be better served. Some parishes may need to modify their catechetical program in order to meet the needs of neophytes.

Initiated for Mission

As newly initiated disciples, children not only participate in ongoing catechetical formation, they also have a role in the ongoing mission of Jesus Christ. The three sacraments of initiation enable the children "to carry out the mission of the entire people of God in the Church and in the world" (*RCIA*, General Introduction, #2). Children, like adults, are initiated into the community of disciples that continues the mission of Jesus Christ and the Church. Though their roles are obviously different from those of adults, children nonetheless are initiated for mission. They are not "just members" of the Church, they are disciples

121

who have a share in the coming of the Reign of God.

Every disciple has a different role to play in the coming of the Reign of God. Adults have a role to play in their workplaces, in service to the Church, in service to the community, in working for justice and peace, in commitment to their family.

Young children help realize the Reign of God by bringing the goodness of God into the marketplace as well. Young children give others a glimpse of God's reign by freely sharing their laughter, joyfulness, innocence, honesty, wonder, playfulness, sincerity and unabashed love.

Older children help bring about God's reign when they are honest, faithful, considerate, respectful and helpful toward friends, family and others.

Children fulfill their commitment to be true disciples when they try to be the best person that God made them to be. They are faithful disciples when they are faithful sisters, brothers, children and grandchildren. They are true disciples when they do their best in school and act justly toward others. In general, when children are faithful to themselves, they are faithful disciples.

On the other hand, some children, particularly adolescents, do have a more specific role to play in the mission of the church. Many teens are involved in work for justice and peace. Some teens regularly minister to the poor and homeless. Also, teens and children often serve as assistants in the religious education program or in the Sunday nursery. Other children serve as lectors, assist at the altar and help in any number of ways throughout the parish. Children are also a part of family service projects and other events at the parish or in the larger community.

Lastly, as children grow in faith and mature, their part in the ongoing mission of Jesus Christ and the Church will also grow and develop. Yet, their beginnings as young neophytes lay the foundation for later involvement in the mission of the Church.

Summary

The period of postbaptismal catechesis, or mystagogy, is a time for young neophytes to reflect on their new life as disciples baptized into the paschal mystery of Jesus' life, death, resurrection and glorification. This happens primarily through their participation in Eucharist, particularly in the Sunday Masses of the Easter season. As new initiates, they should meditate on the gospel, share in the Eucharist and participate in the work of the Church. Reflecting on their experience of sacramental initiation at the Easter Vigil also helps them to deepen their grasp of holy mystery.

The period of mystagogy is the beginning of the child's ongoing conversion. The journey of conversion that is Christian initiation culminates at the Easter Vigil and continues throughout mystagogy and beyond. A child's relationship with Jesus Christ continues to grow deeper after initiation, and catechetical formation helps the child live the life of a true disciple.

Finally, as one initiated into the life and death of Jesus Christ, the child also shares in Jesus' mission. Eucharist, discipleship and mission are the pillars of ongoing mystagogy. The goal of mystagogy is to help the children live as disciples of Jesus committed to his mission and to a life of ongoing conversion.

REFERENCES

[1] Robert D. Duggan, "Mystagogy: The Who? What? When? Why? How?," Beginnings and Beyond Institute packet (Falls Church, Va.: The North American Forum on the Catechumenate, 1995), p. 46.

[2] The notion of a "letdown" after the great momentum that leads to initiation was first suggested to me by Victoria Tufano in a presentation she gave to diocesan directors of Christian initiation, 15-16 May 1991 in Detroit.

[3] Ibid. Tufano suggested mystagogy is a time of transition for neophytes.

[4] Claudia Givinsky of Warren, Michigan, described how some catechists are concerned that neophytes will not be as well-formed in the faith as their peers. In reality, the neophytes often have a better informed and deeper faith life than their peers baptized in infancy.

Notes

Conclusion

Rene was fourteen when she and her sister and brother began the initiation process at St. Margaret Parish. She was almost sixteen when she was initiated at the Easter Vigil. Some years later, after I had moved out of state, I happened to meet Rene's sponsor, Mrs. Jackson. We talked at some length about Rene. Mrs. Jackson was still involved in her life. Rene had overcome a difficult home life and was doing well at Indiana State University. Mrs. Jackson described her as a "beautiful, faith-filled young woman" who was still devoted to her family, active in church, and very successful in school.

Although there is no way to measure how much of an impact the initiation process had on Rene's life, there is little doubt that God's grace was active and working in the journey of initiation that contributed to some extent to Rene's happy and successful life. Rene's journey of conversion included a strengthening of her self-esteem, her self-confidence, and her faith in Jesus Christ. Assuredly, those elements and the ongoing support of a sponsor helped to see her through to college and hopefully beyond.

Each child's story and process of initiation is different. Just as God's grace works in unique and various ways, each child's journey of conversion will be different. Some children will benefit greatly from the process of initiation, as did Rene, and others will "drop out" along the way. Even when children do "drop out" of the parish process of initiation, God remains faithful to the child and family. God continues to call and invite the child. Often, somewhere down the road, the child and family come to the Church once again.

When the family participates in the process of initiation, the entire family will frequently experience conversion. In other cases, the family may not even be involved. The mystery and power of God's grace, active in the process of initiation, cannot be predicted, nor should it be underestimated.

In spite of the fact that conversion cannot be planned or predicted, eight key aspects contribute to the child's journey of initiation.

The Rite of Christian Initiation of Adults is the foundation and point of departure. The Rite provides the vision and the guidelines for the initiation of children of catechetical age. Part I is the norm; the first section of Part II is for children and is an adaptation of Part I. The Rite is the essential text for the initiation of children of catechetical age.

Initiation is a journey of conversion. Conversion to a relationship with Jesus Christ is the goal of the process of initiation. Although catechetical instruction is an important part of the process, the initiation of children of catechetical age is not another catechetical program or a program of sacramental preparation. It is a process of conversion centered in the paschal mystery.

Initiation is family-centered. Parents and siblings are involved in the entire process of initiation. Children are dependent on their family and conversion is family-based. Thus, if possible, parents are central throughout the process.

The liturgical rites are essential to the process of initiation. The major rites of initiation are the culmination of each period and point ahead to the period that follows. The minor rites of the period of the catechumenate and the period of purification and enlightenment are an invaluable means of formation for the children. (The Rite says #98-105 are optional.)

Liturgical catechesis is the primary means of formation throughout the process of initiation. Liturgical catechesis leads to, includes and unpacks afterward the liturgical rites of initiation. Liturgical catechesis includes lectionary-based catechesis and sacramental catechesis. The Sunday Liturgy of the Word, followed by a breaking open the word session and extended catechesis is the normative form of lectionary-based catechesis for the period of the catechumenate.

Initiation is anchored in the community. The entire community is responsible for the initiation of children. In particular, the Sunday assembly itself helps form the candidates. The sponsoring families, sponsors, godparents and companions also play an especially important role in the initiation process. Even though the parent is the ordinary sponsor of the child, sponsoring families or individual sponsors walk with the child and family throughout the process. Godparents and peer companions also support the children throughout the journey.

Children have an innate sense of the holy. Children's ability to ask the "big questions" and their affinity to the divine are always to be respected. An informed and compassionate knowledge of children's spirituality is crucial for team members and others involved with children's initiation.

Children are initiated for mission. Through the process of initiation, children become disciples of Jesus Christ. The journey of conversion is focused more on discipleship than membership.

Remembering and implementing these eight key aspects of initiation for children will help to ensure that a parish is well on its way to an effective process of initiation for children of catechetical age. Even if all the ideals of the Rite of Christian Initiation of Adults are not fully implemented immediately, they can gradually be added as a parish progresses in its initiation ministry. In the words of the late Jim Dunning, the master storyteller and father of initiation ministry, who undoubtedly borrowed the phrase from someone else, "If it's worth doing, it's worth doing badly."

Finally, may those involved in the initiation of children be edified, inspired and empowered by the vision of initiation given in the Rite of Christian Initiation of Adults. For we walk the journey of conversion with the children and their families not as instructors or bystanders, but as fellow disciples on the way. As part of the community of the faithful, we share our own stories, deepen our own faith and further our own conversion by sharing the journey with the children and their families. We are graced to have the awesome privilege of witnessing others coming to Christ.

We are on the threshold of realizing the full potential of the Rite of Christian Initiation of Adults. It has the ability to change parish life as we know it. May the children, who are closer to the holy than we shall ever know, lead the way.

Appendix

Sample Interviews

Samples of three interviews are given here as examples of the types of questions an interviewer would ask of a child and her or his family. Typically, the questions are not asked as bluntly as they are given here, but rather in "conversation style." These are questions I have found to be helpful when I talk with a child and family at each respective interview time. Many of the more delicate questions, such as the ones about marriage, I do not ask directly. I try to obtain the needed information in some way throughout the course of the conversation, or at a later time. Often, the family offers information without being directly asked.

Each interview form needs to be adapted to fit the situation (e.g., parent/child interview, parent only, adolescent, young child) and the style of the interviewer. The samples on the following pages cover the initial interview and the interviews prior to the Rite of Acceptance into the Order of Catechumens and to the Rite of Election.

Initial Interview

Child's name/age _____

Date of birth _____

Child's address _____

Parent/Guardian with whom child lives _____

    Mother's name _____

    Father's name _____

    Stepmother's name _____

    Stepfather's name _____

    Relationship of guardian if other than parent _____

Names/ages of siblings:

_____

_____

_____

_____

Child's school _____

Grade in school _____

(Special needs or services at school) _____

_____

_____

Favorite activities or hobbies: _____

_____

_____

Religious history

Has child been baptized? _____ Yes _____ No

Date of baptism _____

Name of church _____

City/state of baptism _____

Description of baptism (trinitarian formula, water): _____

_____

_____

_____

Names of godparents _____

_____

Has child been confirmed? _____ Yes _____ No

If yes, name and place of church _____

_____

Has child received Eucharist? _____ Yes _____ No

If yes, name and place of church _____

_____

_____

Describe the type of religious formation the child has received (formal and informal):

Describe the child's and family's history of church.

To the child

Tell me what you know of God.

Tell me what you know about Jesus.

Do you know any stories from the Bible? Tell me about some of them.

Why do you want to be baptized (or become Catholic)? Or: How do you feel about baptism/initiation if this is your parent's desire?

Do you know anyone who is Catholic? Anyone from this church? Who?

What kind of questions do you have about God, Jesus or the Church?

To the parent

Why do you want your child to be baptized (become Catholic)?

How does your child feel about being baptized/initiated?

Mother's history

Baptized? _____ Yes _____ No

Baptized in what religious tradition? _____

_____

Present religious affiliation _____

Religious history and/or experience of church _____

_____

_____

_____

Father's history

Baptized? _____ Yes _____ No

Baptized in what religious tradition? _____

Present religious affiliation _____

Religious history and/or experience of church _____

_____

_____

_____

Are child's parents married? _____ Yes _____ No

Divorced? _____ Yes _____ No

Have the child's parents been married more than once? _____ Yes _____ No

Are child's parents married in the Catholic Church? _____ Yes _____ No

Stepmother's and/or stepfather's religious affiliation _____

Do parents or any other children have a desire for baptism/initiation? If yes, please expand.

_____

_____

_____

Questions or concerns? _____

_____

_____

_____

Points to discuss

- Process as journey of faith.
- Centrality of Scripture for formation.
- Family-centered process. Parents' role.
- Liturgical rites.
- Sponsoring families.
- Baptism, Confirmation, Eucharist for full initiation.
- Process is flexible.

Discernment Interview

Rite of Acceptance Into the Order of Catechumens and Rite of Welcoming Candidates

*Note: This "interview" is meant to be a conversation. The questions are conversation starters and need to be adapted for each child, family and interviewer. Read the Rite of Christian Initiation of Adults, #42 and #43, before beginning.

Child's name/age _____

Seeking admission as a _____ catechumen _____ candidate

Other family members who may be celebrating the rite _____

_____

_____

Child's sponsor _____

To the child

What have you most enjoyed about the process of initiation? Why?

What have learned about yourself? Your family? God? Jesus?

Why do you want to become part of this parish community?

Tell me about how you pray.

What kind of changes do you see in yourself? Your family?

What would you like to ask God?

What would you like to ask of this parish?

Would you like to continue to be a part of the initiation process? Why?

To the parent or sponsor

In what ways has the process of initiation made a difference in the life of the child?

In what ways has the process of initiation made a difference in the life of the child's family?

How would you describe the child's relationship with God?

What can this community do to support and encourage the faith life of the child?

Discernment Interview

Rite of Election and Rite of Calling Candidates to Continuing Conversion

*Note: This "interview" is meant to be a conversation. The questions are conversation starters and need to be adapted for each child, family and interviewer. Read the *Rite of Christian Initiation of Adults*, #120, before beginning.

Child's name/age _____

Seeking _____ election or _____ to enter into full communion

Other family members seeking election or to enter into full communion _____

_____

_____

_____

Child's godparent(s) 1) _____

2) _____

Child's parish sponsor _____

To the child

Why do you want to receive the sacraments of initiation?

In what way are you a follower/disciple of Jesus Christ?

Tell me about how you pray.

You have listened carefully to God's word. How is God's word important in your life?

(When applicable, discuss more specific areas of conversion: affective, intellectual, moral, social dimensions.)

To the parent, godparent, sponsor

What are some signs you see that tell you the child is ready for initiation?

Tell me about how the journey of initiation has affected the child. The family.

(When applicable, discuss specific areas of conversion such as affective, intellectual, moral, social dimensions.)

Do you have any reservations or hesitations about the child being initiated?

Notes